CROSS**CURRENTS**
PURSUING SOCIAL JUSTICE AND INTERRELIGIOUS WORK
SINCE 1950

CrossCurrents (ISSN 0011-1953; online ISSN 1939-3881) connects the wisdom of the heart with the life of the mind and the experiences of the body. The journal is operated through its parent organization, the Association for Public Religion and Intellectual Life (APRIL), an interreligious network of academics, activists, artists, and community leaders seeking to engage the many ways religion meets the public. Contributions to the journal exist at the nexus of religion, education, the arts, and social justice. The journal is published quarterly on behalf of the Association for Public Religion and Intellectual Life by the University of North Carolina Press.

The Association for Public Religion and Intellectual Life (formerly ARIL) is a global network of leaders, scholars, and social change agents who explore religious life, engage in intellectual inquiry, and lead ethical action in the world today. Their primary objective, especially through annual summer colloquia and *CrossCurrents*, is to bring together leading voices of our time to advocate for justice and to examine global spiritual and interreligious currents in both historical and contemporary perspectives.

A membership to APRIL includes access to *CrossCurrents* starting with Volume 58, 2008, though our partners at Project MUSE, monthly newsletters, early access to summer colloquium themes, a 40% on UNC Press books, and more. For more information, including membership and subscription rates, visit www.aprilonline.org.

This reissue of *CrossCurrents* was one of four issues published in 2010 as part of Volume 60. For a current masthead visit www.aprilonline.org.

© 2010 Association for Public Religion and Intellectual Life. All rights reserved.

ISBN 978-1-4696-6675-4 (Print)

CROSS CURRENTS

EDITORIAL

4
Theopoetics
Scott Holland

ARTICLES

6
Theopoetry or Theopoetics?
David L. Miller

24
Notes Toward the Heretical Sublime
Jeff Gundy

45
Theopoetics: Si(g)ns of Copulation
Crystal Downing

60
Kavvanah: The Poetry of Blessing and the Blessing of Poetry
David Harris Ebenbach

70
Simone Weil's Ethic of the Other: Explicating Fictions through Fiction, or Looking through the Wrong End of the Telescope
Ruthann Knechel Johansen

89
Divine Exploration and Invitation
L.B.C. Keefe-Perry

105
Theopoetics and Social Change
Matt Guynn

115
A Theopoetics of the Body: Birth, Ecstasy, Emptying, Place, and Death
Patty Christiena Willis

125
Salmoneus and the Poets: Poetry in a World of Violence
Travis Poling

131
Pomegranate
Jean Janzen

POETRY

134
Psalm 91
Jean Janzen

135
Writing the Fire
Jean Janzen

137
Notes on Contributors

On the Cover: The cover image is a painting by
Carrie Patterson
detail, 8 ft. St. Francis Xavier
acrylic and oil on canvas
2008
www.carriepatterson.com

EDITORIAL

Theopoetics

Before the message, the vision; before the sermon, the hymn; before the prose, the poem. The discursive categories of theology as well as the traditional images of sermon and prayer require a theopoetic.

Amos Niven Wilder, *Theopoetic*

Before 1995, the term "theopoetic" was used freely by only a small circle of creative theologians to describe their work: Amos Niven Wilder, Stanley Romaine Hopper, David L. Miller, and Rubem Alves. However, today, simply Google "theopoetics," and you will get scores and scores of hits from Wikipedia to Amazon.com to Facebook postings to the very engaging website, theopoetics.net. One of my young graduate students in a newly developed course, From Theology to Theopoetics, declared, "Theopoetics is the rage!"

Indeed, many theologians and religious writers now find the term, first coined by Stanley Hopper to imagine a kind of theological composition at the end of metaphysics and in face of the death of God, descriptive of their own projects. Merely surfing the Web on the theopoetics wave reveals that Peter Rollins is calling us from theo-logos to theopoetics. Catherine Keller is doing a passionate theopoetics in a revisionist style of process theology. Jack Caputo is writing about the poetics of Jesus as a theopoetics. Richard Kearney is doing it. Melanie May is doing it. This year, the Continental Theology conference at Louvain featured a paper on it, and Roland Faber is reminding us that "God is the poet of the world."

The Summer 2009 issue of *Christianity and Literature* has a very helpful article surveying the emergence and evolution of the genre of theopoetics by L. B. C. Keefe-Perry. This article notes that the reemergence of theopoetics after 1995 was featured in some pieces in *CrossCurrents*, which suggested a movement beyond theology as a metaphysics, systematics, or dogmatics to a poetics because, after all, "the Creator God of Genesis is not a moralist but a poet and a potter." In "Theology is a Kind of Writing: The Emergence of Theopoetics" (*CrossCurrents*, Fall, 1997), I made the case that theopoetics is a kind of writing that invites more writing. Its narratives lead to other narratives, its metaphors encourage new metaphors, its confessions invoke more confessions, and its conversations invite more conversations.

Theology is a kind of writing. What kind of writing is it? Theology in our postmodern condition might be best understood as a poetics, not a metaphysics, for in the rhythms of creation aesthetics precedes ethics. This is not to suggest that all contemporary theology must be written in verse, although that would be lovely indeed. Theopoetics contends that whether theology is inscribed in the genre of poetry, in the form of story, or in a thicker, more theoretical style of prose, it remains a *poiesis*: an inventive, intuitive, and imaginative act of composition performed by authors.

We at *CrossCurrents* are delighted to bring to our readers some of the finest writers in the diverse and evolving genre of theopoetics. David L. Miller, Jeff Gundy, Crystal Downing, David Ebenbach, Ruthann Johansen, Callid Keefe-Perry, Matt Guynn, Patty Willis, Travis Poling, and Jean Janzen give us a more artful and culturally engaged spirituality, theology, and ethics.

The grand nineteenth century preacher, poet, and philosopher Ralph Waldo Emerson grew unhappy with both the moral philosophers and philosophical theologians of his day. He announced that philosophy and theology would one day be taught by poets! Following Emerson's charge that religious writers must work by art rather than by inherited doctrine, the theopoets featured in this issue of the journal offer us poetry, story, and prose embodied in the style and substance of theology as imaginative construction.

–Scott Holland

THEOPOETRY OR THEOPOETICS?

David L. Miller

Introduction: Theopoetics, Theopoetry, and the Death of God

In what may be the most compelling opening sentence of contemporary fiction, Donald Barthelme, in his short-story "On Angels," wrote: "The death of God left the angels in a strange position."[1] To be sure! And one might have thought that the so-called "death of God" would have also created something of an awkwardness for contemporary theology and theologians. But this seems not to have been the case, if one can judge by the trajectory of the movement that has been referred to as theopoetics. At least it seems not to have been the case for all theopoeticians. A quick glance at a website dedicated to theopoetics (http://theopoetics.net) makes the point that for some thinkers identifying themselves with a theopoetics perspective the "death of God" is not at issue while for others it is very much at issue.

The names associated with theopoetics on the Theopoetics.net website prior to 1995 (Rubem Alves, Stanley Hopper, David Miller, Amos Wilder), as well as those associated with theopoetics after 1995 (John Caputo, Thomas Dailey, Jason Derr, Roland Faber, Matt Guynn, Scott Holland, Jean Janzen, L. B. C. Keefe-Perry, Catherine Keller, Melanie May, Travis Poling), by no means make up a uniform group.[2] Radically different discourses, it would seem, parade under the name and aegis of the term "theopoetics." There are doubtless many ways to distinguish the thinking and writing of these various scholars of religion, but one way is to place them in relation to the "death of God" that Barthelme's angels find understandably awkward. For some theopoeticians, the phrase "death of God" seems unimportant and not awkward, and for others the "death of God" is crucial, even if awkward, to the significance of "theopoetics."

This issue of the continuing importance of the "death of God" in religious studies and theology, after its earlier announcement in the 1960s, has recently emerged in reviews of three books by celebrated authors: *Living the Death of God: A Theological Memoir* by Thomas J. J. Altizer, *After the Death of God* by John D. Caputo and Gianni Vattimo, and *After God* by Mark C. Taylor.[3] In her review, Lissa McCullough carefully distinguishes perspectives on the "death of God" represented by these books' authors. For Caputo, it is the "ongoing work of the critique of idols," i.e., the death of finite human views of the infinite divine. For Altizer, the "death of God" is a real death, a final and irrevocable transformation of God. For Taylor, the matter is dialectical and complex, neither a positing of something positive as it is for Caputo nor the positing of something unambiguously negative as it is for Altizer. For Vattimo it is Christendom that has failed (i.e., died) in its lack of charity and love.[4] These differences matter because they imply different functions for the word "after" in two of the books' titles, as Jeffrey Kosky has noted in his review. For example, for Vattimo, and presumably also for Altizer and Taylor, "after the death of God" means "living on in the wake of God," whereas for Caputo "after the death of God" means "we can put the death of God behind us and be nourished anew by the name of 'God.'"[5]

These thinkers do have something in common, according to McCullough. They all may be viewed as "apologists for the vocation of straying toward an infinite nothing, or erring 'after God,' or waiting for the Messiah who never comes, or loving one's neighbor in the void as the only alternative to the bad faith of arbitrarily declared absolutes."[6] But the significant difference is that Caputo, according to Kosky, thinks that "postmodernism is and should be done with the death of God."[7] Whereas Altizer, on the other hand, according to McCullough, believes that "we live in an era when it is thinkable to discuss a 'religion' without rituals and beliefs, a 'faith' purged of religion, a 'theology' without God, and an atheism that is 'an expression of faith itself.'"[8]

The term "theopoetics" will have a different function depending on which significance one gives to the phrase "after the death of God." If one thinks that we should be done with the death of God (or never have entertained the Nietzschean notion in the first place), then theopoetics can refer to an artful, imaginative, creative, beautiful, and rhetorically compelling manner of speaking and thinking concerning a theological knowledge that is and always has been in our possession and a part of our faith. I should like to refer to this perspective as "theopoetry," i.e., as the poetizing of an extant religious faith or theological knowledge. But if one thinks that "after the death of God" signifies the continuing impact of an understanding of the times as severed from any dependencies on transcendental referents, then theopoetics will have to refer to strategies of human signification in the absence of fixed and ultimate meanings accessible to knowledge or faith. I should like to refer to this perspective as "theopoetics," as it involves a poetics and not a poetry, i.e., a reflection on *poiesis*, a formal thinking about the nature of the making of meaning, which subverts the *-ology*, the nature of the logic, of theology.

It is theopoetics and not theopoetry when Altizer writes: "In modernity, it is writers and artists rather than theologians who teach this difficult truth," that "to say Yes to absolute nothingness is to discover plenitude in the void. This fullness in no way represses or forgets the emptiness in the midst of life but allows us to live with an abandon that embraces loss and lack as the very condition of our existence.... Theology ends with the death of God," and Altizer affirms that theopoetics begins when theology ends, even if he does not use the term "theopoetics." Altizer writes[9]: "How ironic that our imaginative vision [i.e., Dante, Milton, Blake, Joyce] should be so richly theological, whereas our theological thinking is so constricted and confined."[10] The philosopher, Simon Critchley, has recently made a point very similar to that of Altizer: "After the death of God, it is in and as literature that the issue of life's possible redemption is played out."[11] And, again, Critchley writes concerning the poet Wallace Stevens: "After one had abandoned a belief in God, poetry is that essence that takes its place as life's redemption."[12] In theopoetry, as opposed to theopoetics, theology does not end with the death of God, because there is no death of God. Theopoetry is just another way of expressing theology's eternal truth. But the initial use of the term "theopoetics" had a different force and function, as can be seen by reference to the discourse concerning theopoetics in the 1960s, not incidentally at the same period of time that witnessed the mid-century "death of God" movement.

History: Stanley Romaine Hopper and the Drew Years (1962–1968)

Amos Wilder, in a book from 1976 whose title is *Theopoetic*, observed: "I believe that I had picked up the term 'theopoetic' and 'theopoiesis' from Stanley Hopper and his students, no doubt in one or another of the remarkable consultations on hermeneutics and language, which he had organized at Drew and at Syracuse to which many of us are indebted."[13] Wilder is alluding to conferences at Drew University in 1962,[14] 1964 and 1966,[15] and a fourth conference at Syracuse University in 1970.[16] These consultations were located intellectually at the intersection of left-wing Bultmannian Biblical interpretation, the thought of the late period of Heidegger's existential philosophy, and the Religion and Literature movement. The first one focused on hermeneutics and Biblical interpretation and featured Gerhard Ebeling and Ernst Fuchs. The second, a follow-up to the first, was more theological, and Fritz Buri and Heinrich Ott made presentations. In the third conference, literary and philosophical perspectives were added and the speakers included Beda Allemann, Owen Barfield, Norman O. Brown, Kenneth Burke, and Julián Marías. And the fourth, following upon the third in theme and perspectives, featured Beda Allemann, Henry Bugbee, Richard DiMartino, Hans Georg Gadamer, Keiji Nishitani, and Wolfgang Zucker.

Because of the centrality of Heidegger's perspective on language and poetry (citing Hölderlin, Heidegger had written, "poetically human beings dwell upon the earth"), Stanley Hopper and Karfried Froelich visited with Heidegger prior to the second consultation and they invited him to be in attendance. He agreed. But because of illness he could not attend. Instead, he sent a letter in which he urged three questions upon the deliberations: (1) what is the nature of the referent of theological utterance; (2) what is the nature of thinking that is objectifying; and (3) is a non-objectivizing thinking and speaking possible?[17]

The problematic of objectivizing discourse is theologically the problem of idolatry and it may well be that all speech reifies its subject in some manner. But it does not follow—or so it was the experiment of these consultations to probe—that language may not be able to perform an entirely different function, namely, to use Heideggerian language, to bring Being to appearance, to allow the unveiling of Truth (*a-letheia*), and to let that which *is* appear *as* that which it is.

The "as" is crucial. Already in *Being and Time*, Heidegger had argued that all language has an *as*-structure. In the third Drew consultation, this led to the implication that theology is not a the-*ology*, but is ineluctably theo-*poetic*, where poetry is interpreted as radical metaphor. Beda Allemann referred to such radical metaphor as "anti-metaphor" or "absolute metaphor,"[18] and Hopper, following Philip Wheelwright, called it "diaphor" as opposed to "epiphor."[19] That is, one is not viewing poetry as mere metaphor, simile without the word "like," which would be the expression of the likeness of like things, ignoring difference. Such a weak reading of the notion of metaphor would constitute a reinscription of objectivization and of the onto-metaphysical tradition in which Being is viewed as *a* being or God as an idol.

Hopper saw this move in the direction of a radical poetic consciousness as "theopoetical," and he wrote, in his introduction to the third consultation: "What *theo-poiesis* does is to effect disclosure through the crucial nexus of events, thereby making the crux of knowing, both morally and esthetically, radically decisive in time."[20] Amos Wilder's reference to Stanley Hopper and the Drew hermeneutics conferences in relation to the early uses of the term "theopoetics" was surely on the mark, and Wilder himself carried on the theopoetical perspective in religious discourse, de-nominalizing, and de-objectivizing theological referents in a manner consistent with apophatic intentionality, i.e., a "speaking away."[21]

But for Hopper de-objectivization of theological discourse is not merely the longstanding and traditional critique of idolatry, though it is that, too. It much more radically marks what others in this period were calling the death of God (e.g., Altizer, Vahanian, Rubenstein, Hamilton). Poetry is no help if the unconscious poetics that accompanies it imagines poetizing to be an adornment, a prettification, a rhetorical strategy that obscures what Hopper already in 1944 had called a "crisis of faith."[22] In his Eranos lecture of 1965, he drew upon the following lines of Wallace Stevens to make his radical point: "The heaven of Europe is empty, like a Schloss/Abandoned because of taxes"; "The steeples are empty and so are the people"; and "It was when I said/'There is no such thing as the truth,'/That the grapes seemed fatter,/The fox ran out of his hole."[23] The problem requires not a turn to uses of poetry and the other arts to bring to expression a traditional theology; rather, the "crisis" of the death of God[24] requires a radicalized poetics in the face of nothingness, i.e., the no-thing-ness of ultimate reality.[25] I should like to attempt to identify four markers of what one might mean by a "radicalized poetics."[26]

Radical Poetics: Four Marks

1. *No Author*. In ancient times when a Muse was given credit for the poetry and when other persons' names were attached to the writing (e.g., *Homeric Hymns, Gospel of Matthew*), and again in modernity in the 1968 essay by Roland Barthes, "Death of the Author," there seems to be a nervousness or suspicion (Harold Bloom's "anxiety of influence" and "clinamen") concerning the real source of poetic texts. Barthes saw the notion of an author, or authorial authority, as the claim of a human intention that comes to be imagined as the meaning of the text. Others called this an "intentional fallacy." But the multiplicity of possible meanings of any poetic text, as well as the inability for anyone to know for certain the state of an author's mind (least of all the author himself or herself) makes this claim untenable.[27] It is difficult to know finally what is the true source of signification in a poem, not least because the signification itself is finally unknown and unknowable. A proper poetics needs to bracket the question of author and authority.

Poets have themselves noted this. For example, this is in part the force of John Keats' notion of the "negative capability" of a good poet. In a letter to his brothers in December of 1817, Keats wrote: "It at once struck me what quality went to form a Person of Achievement, especially in literature and which Shakespeare possessed so enormously—I mean Negative Capability, that is when a person is capable of being in uncertainties, mysteries, doubts without any irritable reaching after fact and reason."[28] A modest "negative capability" will also be reflected in the fact, as I. A. Richards has observed, that "the great writer seldom regards him [or her] self as a personality with something to say; his [or her] mind is simply a place where something happens to words." And Richards adds: "Whatever the author may think that he or she is entitled to do to a poem, the poem has the last word."[29]

That the ego-consciousness of the poet is not in the final analysis authorial is reflected humorously by Oscar Wilde, who wrote, "All bad poetry springs from genuine feeling,"[30] i.e., from the sensibilities of a personal ego. More recently John Ashberry quipped: "There is a view that poetry should improve your life. I think people confuse it with the Salvation Army."[31] Not only is the ego-personality of the author eclipsed by the poem; so also is the ego-personality of the auditor or reader.

Poetry leads to the death of the ego and ego's attitudes, standpoints and beliefs. Or perhaps, more radically, it points to the fact that ego and its cherished notions were illusory (dead) to begin with. Philosophers have talked this way about philosophy for some time. For example, Montaigne wrote that "… to philosophize is to learn how to die. … It is uncertain where death awaits us; let us await it everywhere. Premeditation of death is premeditation of freedom. The one who has learned how to die has unlearned how to be a slave. … The constant work of life is to build death."[32] And, as is well known, Socrates (according to Plato) believed that "those who do philosophy correctly are preparing themselves for death."[33] So it is also with poetry, according to a radical poetics.[34]

2. *No Meaning.* It is a commonplace that poets do not like critics to tell people what their poems mean. The poet's complaint not only has as its rationale that poems have multiple meanings and cannot be limited to singular signification. It may also be linked to the sentiment of Archibold MacLeish in his *"Ars Poetica"*: "A poem should not mean/But be."[35] Poetry and its poetics calls into question the meaning of "meaning," and could be said to have no meaning.[36]

Two depth psychologists have expressed this sensibility. C. G. Jung wrote: "We have talked so much about the meaning of works of art that one can hardly suppress a doubt as to whether art really 'means' anything at all. Perhaps art has no 'meaning,' at least not as we understand meaning. Perhaps it is like nature, which simply *is* and 'means' nothing beyond that…. It needs no meaning, for meaning has nothing to do with art."[37] And more recently, Wolfgang Giegerich, a contemporary Jungian psychologist, extends Jung's psychological point about poetics to the realms of myth and religion. He writes: "There is no need for 'meaning' … for myth or religion as a present reality. On the contrary, we can, now that the gods have become memories, devote ourselves to all the riches of Mnemosyne freely without having to hold our breath in awe.... The feeling that there should be a higher meaning of life and it is missing *is* the illness."[38]

Joseph Campbell dwelt on the issue of the meaning of meaning and meaninglessness in his 1957 lecture at the Eranos Conference in Switzerland. He said: "The world, the entire universe, its god and all, has become a symbol—signifying nothing: a symbol without meaning. For to attribute meaning to any part of it would be to relax its force as a bow, and the arrow of the soul then would lodge only in the sphere of meaning.... The bow, to function as a bow and not as a snare, must have no meaning whatsoever in itself—or in any part of itself—beyond that of being an agent for disengagement—from itself: no more meaning than the impact of the doctor's little hammer when it hits your knee, to make it jerk."[39] Then, to the point, Campbell cited Christian scripture: "Consider the lilies of the fields, how they grow; they toil not, neither do they spin!"[40] And Campbell commented: "What—I ask—is the meaning of a flower? And having no meaning, should the flower then not be?"[41] Campbell ended his lecture in a celebrative mode: "Our meaning is now the meaning that is no meaning.... And if we are to participate joyfully in the world without meaning, we must allow our spirits to become ... wild ganders, and fly in timeless, spaceless flight ... not into any fixed heaven beyond the firmament (for there is no heaven out there), but to that seat of experience simultaneously without and within, where ... the meaninglessness of the sense of existence and the meaninglessness of the meanings of the world are one."[42]

In a lecture at Drew University in the 1960s, I heard the Roman Catholic theologian, William O. Lynch, make a similar point. He was reflecting on the line by T. S. Eliot in *The Four Quartets*: "We had the experience but missed the meaning."[43] Father Lynch countered by suggesting that it may be that we have had so many meanings projected upon us over the years—political, social, religious, and ideological meanings—and that meanwhile we missed the experience of life. This revision by Father Lynch, and the reasoning of Jung, Giegerich, and Campbell, are perhaps not unlike the line of the seventeenth-century mystic, Angelus Silesius: "The rose was without why; it blooms because it blooms. Forgetful of itself, oblivious to our vision."[44] So it is with a blooming poetics: a lot of depth of experience in the poetry; and no meaning, which in the final analysis is the concern of ego. A poem—like a poetic life—must not mean, but be.

3. *No Order (Complexity)*. That poetry does not have single or fixed meaning has led some to argue that the logic of poetry is best understood under the aegis of complexity theory. For example, both Adalaide Morris and Thomas Weissert argue this in a book edited by Katherine Hayles entitled *Chaos and Order: Complexity in Literature and Science*.[45] Weissert notes that the narrative poetics of Jorge Luis Borges in "The Garden of Forking Paths" describes the logic of bifurcation theory thirty years before mathematicians formulated it.

"The Garden of Forking Paths" is a narrative that is labyrinthine, and it is about a man who constructs a narrative (a novel) about a labyrinth which is itself labyrinthine. In the story a man named Albert comments that "in all fictional works, each time a man is confronted with several alternatives, he chooses one and eliminates the others," but in the narrative being considered in Borges' narrative the author "chooses simultaneously all of the alternatives."[46] The narrative plot, its movement through the story's time, thus produces "an infinite series of times, in a growing, dizzying net of divergent, convergent and parallel times. This network of times which approached one another, forked, broke off, or was unaware of one another ..., embraces *all* possibilities of time."[47] Weissert notes the similarity of this presentation of time and motion to that aspect of complexity theory referred to as bifurcation.

Bifurcation theory, for example, traces the logic of a leaf that comes to rest on a stone while floating in a stream. The leaf goes down the stream according to Newtonian laws and its path can be precisely predicted if one knows all of the variables of the stream's motion. But when it comes to rest on a stone, which way it will go next is unpredictable on linear models of cause and effect. So now the theory that applies to its movement is chaos theory. But once the leaf goes one way or the other, it returns to Newtonian orderliness. So, bifurcation theory—one aspect of complexity theory—depicts a logic that is neither completely chaotic nor completely orderly. It shares both characteristics in a single event.[48]

Complexity theory has recently pervaded network theory, meteorology, thermodynamics, quantum mechanics, epidemiology, and now poetics and religious studies. It has been utilized in analyses of traffic jams, terrorism, stock market fluctuation, outbreaks of measles, and growth of cancerous tumors. It is a way of thinking about and imagining any system that is non-linear and difficult to model.[49]

An example of a complex phenomenon is the double pendulum. A normal pendulum has one end fixed and the other end swinging free. When the amount of oscillation is not too large, the pendulum's motion and where it will come to rest (the attractor) can be calculated using linear differential equations. But if a second pendulum is attached at the swinging end of the first pendulum, thus producing a double-jointed structure, the double pendulum still follows Newtonian laws of motion, but in such a fashion that the movement cannot be predicted in linear terms. The phenomenon is now complex.[50] This sort of phenomenon interests complexity theorists. As Ilye Prigogine and Isabelle Stengers wrote: "It is no longer stable situations or permanency that interest us, but rather evolutions, crises, and instabilities."[51] Unpredictability is to be expected.

Neil Johnson itemized eight characteristics of complex phenomena.
1. The system contains a collection of many interacting objects or agents.
2. The behavior of these objects is affected by memory and feedback.
3. They adapt their strategies according to their history.
4. The system is typically open.
5. It appears to be alive.
6. It exhibits emergent phenomena which are generally surprising and may be extreme and self-generated.
7. The emergent phenomena typically arise in the absence of any sort of invisible hand or central controller.
8. The system shows a complicated mix of ordered and disordered behavior, but it tends to move between different arrangements in such a way that pockets of order are created.[52]

This list of characteristics together implies that complex phenomena not only are in a complex that is both orderly and chaotic at once, but also that as the phenomena emerge autonomously they constantly adapt in relation to the lively interaction of the constitutive elements.

Mark C. Taylor has noted that it may be useful to recall the etymology of the word "complexity" in an attempt to understand complexity theory. The term comes from the Latin word *complectere* (also *complexus*), which means "to entwine together," i.e., *com-* ("together") + *plectere* ("to twine or braid"). The stem, *plek* (="to plait"), forms the Latin suffix, *-plex* (="to fold").[53] The point implied by this etymology—as Taylor points out—is that complex systems are not just complicated systems. A snowflake is complicated, but the rules for generating it are simple. The structure of a snowflake, moreover, persists unchanged and crystalline from the first moment of its existence until it melts, while complex systems change over time. It is true that a turbulent river rushing through a narrow channel of rapids changes over time too, but it changes chaotically. The kind of change characteristic of complex systems lies somewhere between the pure order of crystalline snowflakes and the disorder of chaotic or turbulent flow."[54] Complicated is the opposite of simple, whereas complexity is the opposite of independent,[55] because emergent adaptive phenomena autonomously configure in relation to memory and feedback of the elements in the complex.

Complex adaptive systems, being neither completely chaotic nor completely orderly, are unpredictable but not without moments of emerging signification and order. They dwell at the edge of chaos, but not in chaos.[56] Always on an edge, like great poetry. Or as Taylor puts it: "Awareness is always incomplete and hence must forever be refigured. As emergence is aleatory, life is always surprising, plans are frustrated, schemata shattered—who would want it otherwise."[57]

4. *No End (Enjambment)*. The argument about a poetics of complexity leads finally to a fourth point about a radical poetics, a point explored in detail by the Italian postmodern critical theorist Giorgio Agamben: namely, enjambment.[58] What is "enjambment"? The word is from the French term *enjamber*, and is related to the French words *jambe* ("leg") and *jambon* ("ham" or "thigh"). The French verb *enjamber* means "to stride." So enjambment has something to do with the stride or meter of poetry.

Actually "enjambment" is the most common answer to the question of what constitutes the difference between prose and poetry. An obvious difference is that the lines of prose continue to the right margin of the page and the lines of poetry often end before getting to the right margin. Put more technically, enjambment is the opposition of a metrical limit to a syntactical limit, i.e., the rhyme or meter ends without the meaning of the sentence having been completed. Agamben thinks that this is most fundamental and most significant to the poetic function. He notes that Dante, in *De vulgari eloquentia*, already identified this as the basic mark of poetry. Dante was speaking about the notion of *stanza* or "verse" (*versure*), the Latin form of which indicates the point at which a plow turns around at the end of a furrow.[59] Paul Valéry's manner of expressing this poetic distinction was to call poetry "a prolonged hesitation between sound and sense."[60]

If enjambment is the defining characteristic of poetry, then the final line of a poem presents a problem to the author, which is why some poets do not end their final lines with a period (e.g., W. S. Merwin). The problem is that if the last line in a poem is taken to be "final," it is the one line in the poem that is not poetic, i.e., is not enjambed. It does not go on. This is why the last line of a poem is so difficult to construct poetically and to read poetically.

The function of enjambment is to force the eye to the next line. It makes the reader feel a sense of movement and urgency, even disorder. It delays the intention of the line and plays on a reader's expectation. It keeps things going on, often presenting surprise and unpredictability in the turn to the next line of the poem. It prevents fixed and prosaic meanings. It requires the reader to relinquish ego-control and fixations. For example, here is a case of enjambment from a recent poem by W. S. Merwin:

> ...I cherish
> only now a joy I was not aware of
> when it was here although it remains
> out of reach and will not be caught or named
> or called back and if I could I make it stay
> as I want to it would turn into pain[61]

The enjambments turn (*versure*) a joy, when present, into being absent from awareness, and which though it remains, is not within reach, and, while being called back in the poem, cannot be called back, and if it were staying with me now would not be joy at all, but pain. And though we are looking at the last line of "One of the Butterflies," there is no end to the poem. No period. Enjambment keeps things emergent, adaptive, and open. There is not finality or fixity. Nothing is positivized or objectivized, not even the notion of emergent adaptive and open complexity!

Radical Poetics as Theopoetics: Concluding Suggestions

These four marks of a radical poetics are being proposed as a base for understanding a theopoetics in the wake of the death of God. They are not really a ground for a theopoetics, or if they be a ground then they are a groundless ground. The ground has cracked and dropped away. Or as Stanley Hopper often put it late in his life, drawing upon a figure of Nietzsche, the ground is more like an abyss, because there is always "a cavern beneath the cave."[62] The open groundless ground is like Zen's "bottomless pail" or "bottomless basket" whose point is to break through the bottom of the bottom into openness.[63]

The notion of "no author" in a radical poetics implies in theopoetics the death or letting go of the pretension to authorship and authority of the theologian. "No meaning" implies the end of a pretension to the meaningfulness of posited or objectivized theological meanings. "No order"—complexity theory—in a radical theopoetics views religion as disordering as well as ordering, defamiliarizing, questioning, always perceiving religion and religions as complex adaptive emergent complexes. "No end"—enjambment—implies that a criterion of theopoetics is that it generates a next line, a next line that may be unpredictable and containing surprise. Theopoetics is fundamentally iconoclastic, even regarding iconoclasm and itself. It is not to be confused with theopoetry, however, attractive that may seem. Theopoetics makes a more radical challenge to religious discourse and understanding.

If this makes things difficult for conventional theologians and theologies, it is only to the end of siding with the angels in their awkwardness, not only in the wake of the death of God, as Barthelme indicated, but also in the face of the idolatries projected upon them over the years by theological traditions.

Notes

1. Donald Barthelme, "On Angels," *The New Yorker* 45 (August 9, 1969): 29.
2. "THEOPOETICS(dot)NET," http://theopoetics.net/ (accessed June 26, 2009). See the link named "Who?"

3. The reviews alluded to are: Lissa McCullough, "Death of God Reprise: Altizer, Taylor, Vattimo, Caputo, Vahanian," *Journal for Cultural and Religious Theory*, 9/3 (2008): 97–109 (www.jcrt.org); Jeffrey L. Kosky, "Review of After the Death of God by John D. Caputo and Gianni Vattimo, ed. by Jeffrey W. Robbins," *Journal of the American Academy of Religion*, 76/4 (2008): 1021–25; and, John D. Caputo, "Review of After God by Mark C. Taylor," *Journal of the American Academy of Religion*, 77/1 (2009): 162–5.
4. McCullough, "Death of God Reprise," 107.
5. Kosky, "Review," 1024.
6. McCullough, "Death of God Reprise," 108. As Altizer puts it, "As always, our most powerful theology is a negative theology" (Thomas J. J. Altizer, *Living the Death of God: A Theological Memoir* [Albany: State University of New York Press, 2006], p. 125).
7. Kosky, "Review," 1022.
8. McCullough, "Death of God Reprise," 107. See Altizer, *Living the Death of God*, p. 93.
9. Altizer, *Living the Death of God*, p. xvi, xviii. Altizer grounds this view in antiquity, asking: "Why is it not possible to understand the death of God as occurring in the Crucifixion itself? Is the sacrifice of Christ not finally the sacrifice of God"? (106). A Jungian psychologist, Wolfgang Giegerich, has recently made a similar point while writing on the *kenosis* of Jesus as the Christ. "The complete *kenosis* includes the death of God, the loss of 'having' a God altogether. Without the loss of God it would only be a partial or token 'emptying.' And only if he [Jesus as the Christ has lost his God has he really, unreservedly, become human, nothing but human, and emptied his cup fully." Giegerich adds that this implies that "Christianity is the overcoming of *theism* as such." (Wolfgang Giegerich, "God Must Not Die! Jung's Thesis of the One-Sidedness of Christianity," manuscript, forthcoming in the journal *Spring* in the Fall of 2010, used by permission of the author.) The poet Friedrich Hölderlin expressed succinctly the point of Altizer and Giegerich: *Bis Gottes Fehl hilft*, "Sometimes God's absence helps" (*Hölderlin*, tr. M. Hamburger [Baltimore: Penguin Books, 1961], p. 138).
10. Altizer, *Living the Death of God*, p. 42. Compare McCullough, "Death of God Reprise," 101.
11. Simon Critchley, *Very Little … Almost Nothing* (New York: Routledge, 2004), p. xx.
12. Critchley, *Very Little*, p. 115. Critchley recognizes this as a perspective that sounds Romanticist rather than Postmodern and he acknowledges that it represents to some a naïvete. But he urges that one not be naïve about naïvete (pp. 100, 113, 217, 224, 227, and 236).
13. Amos Wilder, *Theopoetic: Theology and the Religious Imagination* (Philadelphia: Fortress Press, 1976), p. iv.
14. The proceedings of this consultation were published in: James Robinson and John Cobb, eds., *The New Hermeneutic* (New York: Harper & Row), 1964.
15. The proceedings of this consultation were published in: Stanley R. Hopper and David Miller, eds., *Interpretation: The Poetry of Meaning* (New York: Harcourt, Brace and World, 1967).
16. For a review of the first three of these consultations, see Stanley R. Hopper, "Introduction," in: Hopper and Miller, eds., *Interpretation*, ix–xxii. Much of what follows in the next paragraphs is indebted to Hopper's account. Cf. David Miller, "Theopoiesis," in: Stanley R. Hopper, *Why Persimmons and Other Poems* (Atlanta: Scholars Press, 1987), 1–12; "Mythopoesis, Psychopoesis, Theopoesis: The Poetries of Meaning" (tape), *Panarion Conference 1976* (Jack Burkee, Box 9926, Marina Del Rey, Calif. 90291); *Christs: Meditations on Archetypal Images*

in *Christian Theology* (New Orleans: Spring Journal Books, 2005); and *Hells and Holy Ghosts: A Theopoetics of Christian Belief* (New Orleans: Spring Journal Books, 2004).

17. Hopper, "Introduction," in: Hopper and Miller, eds., *Interpretation*, p. xiv. This letter, without attribution of its context, appears in Martin Heidegger, *The Piety of Thinking: Essays by Martin Heidegger*, tr. James G. Hart and John C. Maraldo (Bloomington: Indiana University Press, 1976).

18. Beda Allemann, "Metaphor and Anti-Metaphor," in: Hopper and Miller, eds., *Interpretation*, pp. 103–24.

19. Stanley R. Hopper, *The Way of Transfiguration*, R. J. Keiser and T. Stoneburner, eds. (Louisville, KY: Westminster/John Knox Press, 1992), pp. 166, 249, 288–90, 295, 298, 300. See also Philip Wheelwright, *Metaphor and Reality* (Bloomington: Indiana University Press, 1962), pp. 85, 88, 91.

20. Hopper, "Introduction," in: Hopper and Miller, eds., *Interpretation*, p. xix. Compare Hopper's other writings on theopoetics, especially those collected in Hopper, *Way of Transfiguration*, pp. viii, 1–4, 9, 12, 169, 298 and passim. For example: "Theo-logoi belong to the realm of mytho-poetic utterance and... theo-logos is not theologic but theopoesis" (225).

21. The phrase is from Michael Sells, *The Mystical Languages of Unsaying* (Chicago: University of Chicago Press, 1994), and it refers to "negative theology" or "apophatic theology," being Sells' translation of the Greek term *apophasis*, which indicates the impossibility of naming something ineffable.

22. Stanley R. Hopper, *The Crisis of Faith* (Nashville: Abingdon-Cokesbury Press, 1944): "The 'midnight hour' in which 'all men must unmask' is an hour of impotence, solitariness, confusion of Spirit—crisis" (27); [citing Matthew Arnold] "Wandering between two worlds, one dead,/The other powerless to be born,/With nowhere yet to rest my head,/Like these, on earth I wait forlorn" (34); [citing Yeats] "Things fall apart; the center cannot hold;/Mere anarchy is loosed upon the world;/.../The best lack all conviction, while the worst/Are full of passionate intensity" (44); "The critic of culture ... must specify the ambiguities, lay bare the impotence, and beat the bushes of uncertainty until the contradictions everywhere are fully flushed from hiding" (45); etc. Compare Hopper's later work, "The Naming of the Gods in Hölderlin and Rilke," in C. Michalson, ed., *Christianity and the Existentialists* (New York: Charles Scribners and Sons, 1956), which was published twelve years after *The Crisis of Faith*, but still six years before the first Drew conference on hermeneutics, and where the claim is made that the believer (not the unbeliever) must effect that 'willing suspension' not of disbelief but of *belief* in order to let go of a security system that no longer sustains" (154) and where the focus is on the times being defined as *dürftiger Zeit*,"destitute." Concerning this Heideggerian description of the death of God, see Critchley, *Very Little*, pp. 14, 115, 227.

23. Citations are in Stanley R. Hopper, "Symbolic Reality and the Poet's Task," *Eranos-Jahrbuch 34-1965* (Zürich: Rhein-Verlag, 1967), pp. 171 and in "Myth, Dream and Imagination," J. Campbell, ed., *Myths, Dreams and Religion* (New York: Dutton, 1970), p. 112.

24. This crisis of the "death of God" is at base a postmodern epistemological matter, as is indicated by Paul Kugler's mapping of the demise of "transcendental signifiers." Kugler observes, with Sausurre, that "there is no fixed point outside particular systems of

meaning relations, no transcendental referent ...." (*The Alchemy of Discourse* [Einsiedeln: Daimon Verlag, 2002], p. 105). In another essay, Kugler writes about the "twilight of our god-terms" (e.g., truth, reality, center, self, unconscious, soul, wholeness, unity, origin, wish, energy, etc.), and he says: "The more we attempt linguistically to account for the authority of these ultimates, the more the absoluteness in our god-terms begins to deliteralize, dissolve, and disappear. ... all systems of interpretation gain their authority through a grounding in a god-term, a transcendental 'ultimate,' but this 'ultimate is no longer so absolute, so ultimate" (*Raids on the Unthinkable* [New Orleans: Spring Journal Books, 2005], pp. 36, 37). Simon Critchley makes an epistemological point similar to that of Kugler's: "... the possibility of a belief in God or some God-equivalent, whether vindicable through faith or reason has decisively broken down.... Such a thinking does not only entail the death of God of the Judaeo-Christian tradition, but also the death of all those ideals, norms, principles, rules, ends, values that are set above humanity to order to provide human beings with a meaning to life" (*Very Little*, p. 3). Nietzsche referred to "transcendental signifiers" as "the big words" (see Critchley, *Very Little*, p. 11).

25. It is just this distinction between theopoetry as an apologetic for theology and theopoetics grounded in the death of God that marks a principle difference in the Chicago school of Theology and Literature and the Drew school of Religion and Literature. For an instantiation of this division see the engagement of Stanley R. Hopper by Nathan A. Scott, Jr., in the *American Academy of Religion*, 42/2 (1974): 203–31; and Stanley R. Hopper's response, "W. H. Auden and the Circumstance of Praise," *Journal of the American Academy of Religion*, 43/2 (1975): 135–52.

26. These in many ways resemble, but are not precisely the same as the markers of a postmodern consciousness, according to the argument of Mark C. Taylor in *Erring: A Postmodern A/theology* (Chicago: University of Chicago Press, 1984), Part One. Taylor's marks are: 1. The death of God; 2. The Disappearance of the Self; 3. The End of History; and 4. The Closure of the Book.

27. See the Wikipedia article on Roland Barthes at http://en.wikipedia.org/wiki/Roland_Barthes (accessed June 30, 2009).

28. John Keats, *Letters* (December 21, 1817), ed. M. Forman (New York: Oxford University Press, 1948), p. 72.

29. I. A. Richards, "How Does a Poem Know When It Is Finished? In: Daniel Lerner, ed., *Parts and Wholes* (New York: Free Press of Glencoe, 1963), p. 169 (Richards is quoting Northrop Frye). The perspective that the force of the poem comes out of the language rather than out of a person is also expressed by Martin Heidegger, when he writes: *Der Sprache spricht. Der Mensch spricht, insofern er der Sprache entspricht*, i.e., "Language speaks. Man speaks in that he responds to language." (Martin Heidegger, *Unterwegs zur Sprache* [Pfullingen: Verlag Neske, 1975], pp. 32–33; Martin Heidegger, *Poetry, Language, Thought*, tr. A. Hofstadter [New York: Harper and Row, 1971], p. 210).

30. Oscar Wilde, "The Critic as Artist," *The Complete Works*, vol. 4, ed. J. Guy (New York: Oxford University Press, 2007), p. 195.

31. Cited by Francis X. Clines, "Inaugural Poetry: The Ode Not Taken," *New York Times*, editorial section (January 19, 1997), p. 5.

32. Michel de Montaigne, *The Complete Essays of Montaigtne*, tr. D. Frame (Garden City, NY: Anchor Books, 1960), vol. I, pp. 74, 81, 88.
33. Plato, *The Great Dialogues of Plato: Phaedo*, tr. W. H. D. Rouse (New York: New American Library, 1956), pp. 466–67, 485 (64a4-6, 81a11).
34. One could argue the same for depth psychology (as opposed to ego- or humanistic-psychology). Jung, for example, quite late in his life, wrote: "Every advance for the Self is experienced as a defeat [he could have said death] for the ego" (C. G. Jung, *Collected Works*, 14.778), and Wolfgang Giegerich has more recently insisted on the same: "Psychological discourse ... has to be as the negation of the ego, and the psychologist ... has to speak as one who has long died as ego personality. The art of psychological discourse is to speak as someone already deceased" (*The Soul's Logical Life* [Frankfurt: Peter Lang, 1998], p. 24, compare pp. 17, 19, 31).
35. Archibald MacLeish, "Ars Poetica," in: John Ciardi, *How Does a Poem Mean?* (Boston: Houghton Mifflin Company, 1959), p. 909.
36. On this issue, see David L. Miller, "Prometheus, St. Peter, and the Rock: Identity and Difference in Modern Literature," *Eranos 57-1988* (Frankfurt: Insel Verlag, 1990), 75–124.
37. C. G. Jung, *The Spirit in Man, Art and Literature (Collected Works,vol. 15)*, (New York: Pantheon, 1966), paragraph 121.
38. Wolfgang Giegerich, "The End of Meaning and the Birth of Man," *Journal of Jungian Theory and Practice*, 6/1 (2004): 28.
39. Joseph Campbell, "The Symbol without Meaning," *The Flight of the Wild Gander* (Novato, CA: New World Library, 2002), p. 143.
40. Joseph Campbell, "Symbol without Meaning," p. 148.
41. Joseph Campbell, "Symbol without Meaning," p. 152.
42. Joseph Campbell, "Symbol without Meaning," pp. 154–55.
43. T. S. Eliot, "Four Quartets: The Dry Salvages," *The Complete Poems and Plays: 1909–1950* (New York: Harcourt, Brace and Company, 1952), p. 133.
44. Angelus Silesius, *Cherubinic Wanderer*, 1.289. See Angelus Silesius, *The Cherubinic Wanderer*, tr. M. Shrady (New York: Paulist Press, 1986), p. 54. I have modified the translation. The key phrase, *sonder waeromme*, "without why," was a common motif of Medieval mysticism, as Shrady points out in her footnote.
45. Katherine Hayles, ed., *Chaos and Order: Complex Dynamics in Literature and Science* (Chicago: University of Chicago Press, 1991).
46. Jorge Luis Borges, *Labyrinths*, tr. D. Yates (New York: New Directions, 1964), p. 26.
47. Borges, "Garden," p. 28.
48. Thomas Weissert, "Representation and Bifurcation: Borges' Garden of Chaos Dynamics," in Hayles, ed., *Chaos and Order*, pp. 223–243.
49. Two useful sources introducing complexity theory are: Neil Johnson, *Two's Company, Three Is Complexity* (Oxford: One World, 2007); and Mark C. Taylor, *The Moment of Complexity: Emerging Network Culture* (Chicago: University of Chicago Press, 2001).
50. See Hayles, ed., *Chaos and Order*, pp. 8–10.
51. Cited in http://www.connected.org/is/prigogine.html, "The Networked Society," (accessed December 15, 2008).
52. Johnson, *Two's Company, Three Is Complexity*, pp. 13–16.

53. Taylor, *The Moment of Complexity*, p. 138.
54. Taylor, *The Moment of Complexity*, p. 142.
55. See the Wikipedia article on "Complexity," at http://en.wikipedia.org/wiki/Complexity (accessed on December 15, 2008).
56. Taylor, *Moment of Complexity*, pp. 14, 16, 23, 134, 146, 185, and 191. See also Helene Shulman Lorenz, *Living at the Edge of Chaos: Complex Systems in Culture and Psyche* (Einsiedeln: Daimon Verlag, 1997).
57. Mark C. Taylor, *After God*, p. 346.
58. Giorgio Agamben, *The End of the Poem*, tr. D. Heller-Roazen (Stanford, CA: Stanford University Press, 1999), pp. 109–111.
59. Agamben, *End of the Poem*, p. 111.
60. Cited in Agamben, *End of the Poem*, p. 109.
61. W. S. Merwin, "One of the Butterflies," *The Shadow of Sirius* (Port Townsend, WA: Copper Canyon Press, 2008), p. 91.
62. Stanley R. Hopper, "Ontology as Utterance, or The Cavern Beneath of the Cave," manuscript of a presentation given at the Fourth Consultation on Hermeneutics at Syracuse University in 1970; and, "Once More: The Cavern Beneath the Cave," D. R. Griffin, ed., *Archetypal Process* (Evanston, IL: Northwestern University Press, 1989), pp. 107–24. The allusion in these titles is to a saying by Nietzsche in *Beyond Good and Evil*, #289: "In the writings of a hermit one always also hears something of the echo of the desolate regions, something of the whispered tones and the furtive look of solitude; in his strongest words, even in his cry, there still vibrates a new and dangerous kind of silence—of burying something in silence. When a man has been sitting alone with his soul in confidential discord and discourse, year in and year out, day and night; when in his cave—it may be a labyrinth or a gold mine—he has become a cave bear or a treasure digger or a treasure guard and dragon; then even his concepts eventually acquire a peculiar twilight color, an odor just as much of depth as of must, something incommunicable and recalcitrant that blows at every passerby like a chill.... behind every cave in him there is ..., and must necessarily be, a still deeper cave; ... an abyss behind every bottom, beneath every 'foundation.'" (Friedrich Nietzsche, *Beyond Good and Evil*, tr. W. Kaufmann [New York: Vintage, 1966], pp. 228–29) Hopper writes in the 1970 essay: "If we spring away from the idea of a ground in which every being as such is grounded, do we not spring into such an abyss? or into the cavern beneath the grotto beneath the hollow beneath the cave?" (ms. p. 22).
63. From "Transmission of the Lamp" (China, 7th century CE): "All hindrances to the attainment of bodhi which arise from passions that generate karma are originally non-existent. Every cause and effect is but a dream. There is no triple world which one leaves, and no bodhi to search for. The inner reality and outer appearance of man and ten thousand things are identical. The great Tao is formless and boundless. It is free from thought and anxiety." Tao-hsin (4th patriarch, China) "It is like a pail of water when the bottom has fallen away. When nothing retains the water and it has all dropped, the negation is indeed complete." Or from the Zenrin Kushu (Ruth Fuller Sasaki trans.): "In the bottomless bamboo basket I put the white moon; In the bowl of mindlessness I store the pure breeze." http://viewoftheblue.com/frankspage/zenquo.html (accessed July 8, 2009).

NOTES TOWARD THE HERETICAL SUBLIME

Jeff Gundy

A tremendous energy comes from the sense of transgression, especially when coupled with the ethical sense that one's transgressions, although "heresies" to the established order, are acts of faithfulness to a higher power. Whether the sense of transgression or faithfulness is the more powerful driver—a question whose answer seems less than clear to me—it *is* clear that such energy has fueled movements and martyrs throughout history. Some of these transgressors take on the status of heroes, and others remain condemned to villain status... all depending on the outcomes. They include the original followers of Jesus and rebels and reformers all through the church history, as well as poets of all sorts, especially romantics like Blake, Keats, Whitman, and Dickinson, and neo-romantics like Wallace Stevens. Different as these poet and movements are, all are conscious of their transgressions against orthodoxy, and all are convinced they are being true to some more authentic spirit, reality, and/or experience.

Anabaptism, although its paradigms are obviously, even radically anti-Romantic, contains its own heretical imperative in its call to a utopian purity that requires constant renewal and resistance to "the world." The first Anabaptist rebels, with their manifestos, their baptizing of adults, their refusal of oaths, their breaking of images, their rejection of state churches whether Catholic or reformed, were similarly driven by the conviction that most people had gone terribly astray, and drastic changes were needed to set things right. Of course they were heretics according to the established order, and it took them generations to secure their own tiny establishments in the crevices and ravines of that order, to solidify their refusals, negations, and drastic gestures into a new order of their own.

But, as the revolutionary moment gives way to the daily, then monthly and yearly rigors of community survival, the revolutionary order must evolve into order of another sort—and must eventually come to seem a new oppression to a new generation of rebels. As has been adequately documented and dramatized by many artists and writers, Anabaptism has been no less prone than any other sect become establishment to its own institutional hierarchies and oppressions. Along with participation in the general suppression of women and minorities, Mennonite communities have often been particularly suspicious about artistic expressions not confined to a narrow range of pious and/or utilitarian forms. (See my *Walker in the Fog,* passim.)

Especially for the Swiss Brethren Anabaptists and their American descendants, this shift might be seen, very broadly, as a move toward a "heretical pastoral"—a perhaps brash renaming of the "quiet in the land" syndrome, in which Mennonites and Amish sought to preserve difference and purity through withdrawal and to establish rural communities where their radical ideas might be lived out with minimal interference. An important variant, which often ran alongside the withdrawal motif, was the eventual negotiation of toleration and varying degrees of cooperation and mutual exchange between Anabaptists and their neighbors. Especially in the Low Countries, in Poland and Prussia, some developed extensive involvements in their wider communities, often trading a measure of assimilation for greater security and prosperity.[1]

My main interest here, however, is not with church history, but with that edge where religious and poetic energies intersect in the drive to imagine and bring into being another world through the language of poetry. In this sphere, poetry and theology become close companions—some would say competitors—and the relatively new field of "theopoetics" offers useful means of exploring some of the varieties of what I will call the heretical sublime.

The founder of theopoetics, Stanley Hopper, argues that while there is a natural tension between poetry and theology when both claim the right to insights into the ultimate nature of things, it makes little sense to resolve this tension in favor of theology. Instead, Hopper insists that poetry is the primary discipline, because it is open to psychological and existential depths and mysteries, while standard theology is fixated on logic and reason:

> [W]hen we name the conditions of reality by way of the analytical reason, the soul in its movements returns tautologically upon the circle of definitions it sets out with; likewise our symbolic representations may close us in upon the arc of return implicit in their initial figurations. "If I paint the glass blue." says Alan Watts, "I cannot see the sky." And this would be true even though I call the glass the "sky." When I become aware that it is a glass, I must then shatter the glass as a barrier, in order that I may be open to the sky. (125-6)

Hopper quotes approvingly Kafka's aphorism about the need to accomplish the *negative*, claiming that when we confront all that we do not and cannot know about God, we must also acknowledge how inadequate reason and evidence are to the ultimate questions posed by life. We must recognize, Hopper thinks (following many postmodern theorists) that all knowledge is constructed out of language but that language itself is built up out of nothing, out of difference and metaphor, and that all of our discourse about ultimate questions is itself metaphorical (155). Once we do so, he claims, we will naturally turn to the form of discourse most at home in metaphor—poetry—to explore the questions that theology has traditionally claimed as its domain.

This argument has some connections to Mennonite theologian Gordon Kaufman's claim that theology is always a "constructive" human activity and must be recognized as such, although the details of Kaufman's project are quite different than those of Hopper's. Kaufman dismisses most of traditional theology as the product of the over-reification of metaphors like "lord," "father," and "creator"; God, he insists, is far beyond any such human constructions. The most accurate, best metaphor for God, he argues, is "serendipitous creativity," not lord or father or creator:

> What could we possibly be imagining when we attempt to think of God as an all-powerful personal reality existing somehow before and independent of what we today call "the universe"? As far as

> we know, personal agential beings did not exist, and could not have existed, before billions of years of cosmic evolution of a very specific sort, and then further billions of years of biologic evolution also of a very specific sort, had transpired. How then can we today think of a person-like creator-God as existing before and apart from any such evolutionary developments? (54)

Despite the apparent congruence of this argument with Hopper's claims for poetry, Kaufman's affinities to Hopper and theopoetics go only so far. Kauffman understands "creativity," in particular, as a much broader category encompassing all sorts of material and intellectual activity, from the development of planets and life to the writing of theology and of sonnets. Generally, he is still committed to rationalism—he remains a theologian, however innovative and iconoclastic—and suspicious of the intuitive processes of poetry. If God is indeed serendipitous creativity, however, it would seem to follow that in creativity, we all take part in the work of God. This divinity is within us, although we do not have easy access to it, any more than we can reach within and squeeze a few extra drops of bile from our livers when it might be convenient.

Stanley Hopper, in contrast, turns precisely to poetry in hopes of the large-scale transformation he sees as necessary. "When language fails to function at the metaphorical or symbolic levels," he writes, "the imagination goes deeper, soliciting the carrying power of archetype, translating the archetype from the spent symbolic system into fresh embodiments" (220).

The aim of poetry, then, is not to render or describe or narrate—but to discover a language adequate to being, to bring into this world things made of words that draw us toward the full consciousness of which we can yet only dream. This purpose, Hopper argues, is prior to and independent of any other function that a poem might have (although a poem may have many other functions as well). And this purpose is also not subject to limits imposed by other realms of human endeavor. In and of itself, then, Hopper claims poetry of the sort he favors is a holy activity, and not to be circumscribed or contested, although of course the success of its execution remains open to discussion and judgment.

Like Kaufman, Hopper believes that the largest errors of conservative religion are over-reification and misplaced trust in unexamined metaphor. To claim that the language of the past is sufficient to carry God's project into the future, and to claim that God can be contained in human language in ways sufficient to answer all the important human questions, including who is worthy of salvation and who is not, no longer will suffice. New language, new images, new metaphors are constantly required. The quest is not for an absolute naming or a set of propositions that will make of the Divine a comprehensible system—any such project, Hopper believes, is mistaken in its quest for a certitude that is existentially unavailable to us.

What, then? Hopper turns to the work of Martin Heidegger, who himself looks to the poet Rainer Maria Rilke for a way of addressing ultimate questions. In a letter of August 11, 1924, Rilke writes:

> To me it seems more and more as though our customary consciousness lives on the tip of a pyramid whose base within us (and in a certain way beneath us) widens out so fully that the farther we find ourselves able to descend into it, the more generally we appear to be merged into those things that, independent of time and space, are given in our earthly, in the widest sense worldly, existence. (qtd. in Heidegger, *Poetry* 128-9)

How much *can* we know, and how clearly can it be expressed? If knowledge were a simple thing, surely there would be less discourse and more clarity. A main principle of theopoetics is that the mysteries of existence—and what we call God is surely the greatest of these mysteries—can be approached only with proper respect for their nature *as* mysteries. Heidegger speaks of the need to address mystery without reductionism: "But we never get to know a mystery by unveiling or analyzing it; we only get to know it by carefully guarding the mystery *as* mystery. But how can it be carefully guarded—this mystery of proximity—without even being known?" (*Existence* 279-80).

Theology seeks closure and clarity; poetry resists them, resting more readily in uncertainty and incompleteness. Keats's oft-cited idea of "Negative Capability" is relevant: "that is, when a man is capable of being in uncertainties, mysteries, doubts, without any irritable reaching after fact and reason" ([21 Dec. 1817]). Also relevant is this section of Robert Bly's "Six Winter Privacy Poems," "Listening to Bach":

> Inside this music there is someone
> Who is not well described by the names
> Of Jesus, or Jehovah, or the Lord of Hosts! (*Selected Poems,* 57)

The idea that God is unknowable in essential ways is a comfort to many poets, a bitter spur and fundamental challenge to (most) theologians. Theology, at least in its traditional senses, must operate as if a great many things about God can be articulated in human language, or give up its entire enterprise; poets (I might claim) are often able to rest more easily and alertly within the mystery and receive and offer different sorts of information as a result.

Intriguingly, Hopper mistrusts the modernist poetry of both T. S. Eliot—too orthodox—and William Carlos Williams—too secular. Instead, he is a surprising advocate of their contemporary Wallace Stevens. Although Stevens is famous for his abandonment of conventional Christian faith, Hopper finds in his "sense of the dropping away of the entire symbolic world of Christendom" a radical, refreshing opening toward something else: "divinity must be within the world as given," Hopper says, "not superimposed from above or deferred to something remote and static" (70); "The universe that Stevens cannot find a center in is itself that box of the guitar whose emptiness becomes a Presence when we play things as they are" (81).

This emphasis on embodiment and mystery, on presence and materiality as prior to other orders of knowing, allows a fresh look at traditional Anabaptist (and more broadly Christian) claims. To choose one not-quite-random example, we might consider Mennonite theologian John Howard Yoder's essentially orthodox assertion that "The church precedes the world epistemologically. We know more fully from Jesus Christ and in the context of the confessed faith than we know in other ways. . . the meaning and validity and limits of concepts like 'nature' and 'science' are best seen not when looked at alone but in the light of the confession of the lordship of Christ" (*Priestly Kingdom,* 11).

When Yoder writes "the church," he means something like "the church's claims about the nature of things." Christians must, surely, privilege the "knowing" associated with "Jesus Christ and the context of the confessed faith" above other sorts of knowing. And yet, looked at only slightly differently, even "the confession of the lordship of Christ" is a *human* action. Those familiar with Yoder know that he is often dismissive of mystery and mystification; he insists on viewing other practices such as baptism and communion not as "sacraments" whose true significance is in some hidden, miraculous transformation, but as what he calls "ordinary human behavior." They are, he insists, "not mysterious. No esoteric insight is needed for them to make sense. A social scientist could watch them happening" (*Body Politics* 44). Yoder is equally dismissive of "mere poetry," which he seems to consider frivolous at best and dangerous at worst; although he rarely speaks of it directly or at length, in "Armaments and Eschatology," he makes a passing but dismissive reference: "To sing 'The Lamb Is Worthy to Receive Power,' as did the early communities whose hymnody is reflected in the first vision of John, is *not mere poetry*. It is performative proclamation. It redefines the cosmos in a way prerequisite to the moral independence which it takes to speak truth to power. . ." (*Body Politics* 53, emphasis added).

Yoder's rhetoric here reveals a fascinating gap. What he celebrates as "performative proclamation" rather than "mere poetry" seems to me, precisely, the power of poetry to "redefine the cosmos" through language. Such language lays claims whose value as propositional truth finally matters less than their outcomes: it allows, even creates, "the moral independence which it takes to speak truth to power." Thus, the difference between Yoder's view and the other I am trying to trace may be less than first appears; at the least, surely one is not "religious" and the other something else, for both see language as a means of creating change in the world—or, in other words, as a form of power.

Just how primary, then, are intellectual belief-constructions like "the confessed faith?" Does the abstract language of belief precede or hold sway over other forms of language, other mediations between experience and meaning? As Yoder suggests almost despite himself, the performative language of hymns, in which theological assertions are embedded in metaphor and music, often has a force that "mere theology" lacks. Language and cosmos, many believe, are intricately related. Again, Heidegger: "Only where there is language is there world, i.e. the perpetually altering circuit of decision and production, of action and responsibility, but also of commotion and arbitrariness, of decay and confusion. . . . Language is not a tool at his disposal, rather it is that event which disposes of the supreme possibility of human existence. . .

The being of man is founded in language. But this only becomes actual in *conversation*" (*Existence* 300-01).

How *does* language function to structure and shape our perceptions and understandings? Heidegger (and much postmodern thinking after him) assigns language a primary role in consciousness. The poet and critic Anne Carson further notes that in this role, language is deeply interwoven with human intention and desire: "It is nothing new to say that all utterance is erotic in some sense, that all language shows the structure of desire at some level" (108). Any linguistic exchange, she suggests, involves a "symbolic intercourse": "writer and reader bring together two halves of one meaning, so lover and beloved are matched together like two sides of one knucklebone" (108). Not only is desire inseparable from language, but so is imagination: "Imagination is the core of desire. It acts at the core of metaphor. It is essential to the activity of reading and writing" (Carson *Eros*, 77).

Theologians and church authorities—especially since the Reformation—have often sought to keep imagination and desire out of the church because their church is built on Reason and authority, neither of which can survive imagination and desire. This suspicion goes all the way back to Plato, who banned the poets from his Republic because he knew that those informed by imagination would not yield willingly to the rule of reason and authority. But if there is no language *without* desire, without imagination, this prohibition can only lead to disaster.

Anabaptism, perhaps even more than other strains of Christianity, relies on reasoning closely from biblical texts, especially those offering the life and teaching of Jesus, to particular behaviors and practices; in this, it is very much an Enlightenment project. One can celebrate its main projects—especially the drive to make Jesus' nonviolence a norm, not to be rationalized away when it seems necessary to kill somebody or other—while sensing a certain lack of imaginative spaciousness within it.

If the positive heresy of Anabaptism in the context of Christendom is that following Jesus is more important than doing the business of the state and the "world," its most problematic aspect may be its iconoclasm, its mistrust of beauty and the arts and the imagination. Let us turn now to look more closely at the transgressive energy of some particular expressions of the heretical sublime.

II.

At the end of my sophomore year in college, I took a summer course called "Tradition and the Individual Talent." The title came straight from the famous essay by T.S. Eliot, who despite the radical innovations of his poetry was hardly a revolutionary in other spheres; he famously described himself in the preface to *For Lancelot Andrewes* as "classicist in literature, royalist in politics, and anglo-catholic in religion." But the course had been hijacked by the rebel poet-teacher Nicholas Lindsay; while we read Eliot, we spent more time with others such as William Blake (to whom Eliot condescended mercilessly, as I will discuss below), William Butler Yeats, and Theodore Roethke, all of them far more open than Eliot to unconventional approaches to mystery.

What was Blake's project? His ambitions were immodest, to say the least, although the invocation to his prophetic book *Jerusalem* is a blend of the traditional and the unorthodox:

> I rest not from my great task!
> To open the Eternal Worlds, to open the immortal Eyes
> Of Man inwards into the Worlds of Thought, into Eternity
> Ever expanding in the Bosom of God, the Human Imagination.
> O Saviour pour upon me thy Spirit of meekness and love!
> Annihilate the Selfhood in me: be thou all my life. (*Jerusalem* pl. 5; 309)

Worlds of thought, eternity, the Bosom of God, and the human imagination: all are somehow equivalent, or at least interchangeable, in Blake's rhetoric. A main opposition, as he sees it, involves "Abstract Philosophy warring in enmity against Imagination/(Which is the Divine Body of the Lord Jesus, blessed for ever.)" (pl. 5, 311). Blake mistrusted priests and (like a good Anabaptist, although as far as I know he knew nothing about them) saw the collusion of church and state as a betrayal of both. Thus the shocking dystopian vision of "London":

> How the chimney-sweeper's cry
> Every blackening church appalls,
> And the hapless soldier's sigh
> Runs in blood down palace-walls. (44)

In "The Garden of Love," churchly authority is just as shockingly linked to repression and denial; the chapel in this garden has "'Thou shalt not' writ over the door," and instead of flowers, there are graves and tombstones, among which "priests in black gowns were walking their rounds,/And binding with briars my joys and desires" (43).

I loved many things in Blake and was baffled by just as many more. But the single text that struck me most deeply, and which I have returned to many times since, is *The Marriage of Heaven and Hell*. This strange work, a sort of fantastic, composite narrative incorporating long sections of aphorisms and epigrams, is frankly heretical, or at least radically revisionist:

> Without Contraries is no progression. Attraction and Repulsion, Reason and Energy, Love and Hate are necessary to Human existence.
> From these contraries spring what the religious call Good & Evil. Good is the passive that obeys Reason. Evil is the active springing from Energy.
> Good is Heaven. Evil is Hell. (124)

This is Blake's signature voice, or one of them: brusque, dismissive of "the religious" and "the passive that obeys Reason," bent on a project entirely his own.[2] Rehabilitating what "the religious" dismiss as "evil," Blake offers these further grand generalizations as "THE VOICE OF THE DEVIL":

All Bibles or sacred codes have been the causes of the following Errors.
1. That Man has two real existing principles Viz: a Body & a Soul.
2. That Energy, call'd Evil, is alone from the Body, & that Reason, call'd Good, is alone from the Soul.
3. That God will torment Man in Eternity for following his Energies.
   But the following Contraries to these are True:
1. Man has no Body distinct from his Soul, for that called Body is a portion of Soul discerned by the five Senses, the chief inlets of Soul in this age
2. Energy is the only life and is from the Body and Reason is the bound or outward circumference of Energy. (124)

Strong stuff, indeed, for a farm boy not yet twenty. It hardly struck me as something I could "believe," yet the sense of authority was undeniable. And somehow, it seemed strangely plausible, at least in comparison to all those bland exhortations toward goodness I had dutifully absorbed—which seemed strangely inadequate in their accounts of "evil" to so many of us who grew up in the sixties. Richard Nixon claimed to be fighting evil, Jim Morrison did not, but I knew which one's voice I wanted to hear. Blake only gets better: "Those who restrain desire do so because theirs is weak enough to be restrained, and the restrainer or reason usurps its place and governs the unwilling. And being restrained, it by degrees becomes passive till it is only the shadow of desire" (124-5).

Balance between contrary forces is essential, Blake insists—Reason is not bad in itself but has enthroned itself unjustly and painted Energy as the incarnation of evil (in much the way, to add some anachronistic examples, that Captain Ahab did with Moby Dick, and the Bush administration did with any who dared oppose them). As a means of restoring this balance, the Devil gets all the good lines in Blake's version, beginning with this great post- or pre-rational question:

> How do you know but ev'ry Bird that cuts the airy way,
> Is an immense world of delight, clos'd by your senses five? (126)

A later dialogue between this devil and an angel is even more startling. The devil insists that Jesus himself broke all the commandments:

> did he not mock at the sabbath, and so mock the sabbaths God? murder those who were murder'd because of him? turn away the law from the woman taken in adultery? steal the labor of others to support him? bear false witness when he omitted making a defence before Pilate? covet when he pray'd for his disciples, and when he bid them shake off the dust of their feet against such as refused to lodge them? I tell you, no virtue can exist without breaking these ten commandments. Jesus was all virtue, and acted from impulse, not from rules. (136)

The text concludes with a prophetic "Song of Liberty," imagining the collapse of the empire of Reason and the restoration of balance, and ending with this lovely coda:

> Let the Priests of the Raven of dawn, no longer in deadly black, with hoarse note curse the sons of joy. Nor his accepted brethren, whom, tyrant, he calls free: lay the bound or build the roof. Nor pale religious lechery call that virginity, that wishes but acts not!
> "For every thing that lives is Holy." (138)

In this lyrical outburst, Blake presses toward both animism and antinomianism. If every thing is holy, why should some rule over others; why should any obey another? Although Blake was too solitary to be interested in forming a movement, such visionary energy has fueled many rebellions and social experiments. The red-letter cautionary example for Anabaptists has always been what happened at the small north German city of Münster in 1534-5, when a band of apocalyptic Anabaptists took over for over a year and attempted to create a visionary community. Constantly besieged by surrounding armies, with food and able-bodied men in short supply, the leaders eventually resorted to polygamy and public beheadings in the town square in their attempts to hold power. Mennonites have feared such anarchic wildness ever since—and spent centuries trying to deny that such excesses were the natural outcomes of their views.

But might there be a pacifist antinomianism, one in which the only rule is love? The traditionalist answer, unsurprisingly, is "of course not." This perspective is neatly captured by T.S. Eliot's suavely condescending remarks about Blake:

> We have the same respect for Blake's philosophy... that we have for an ingenious piece of home-made furniture: we admire the man who has put it together out of the odds and ends about the house.... Blake was endowed with a capacity for considerable understanding of human nature, with a remarkable and original sense of language and the music of language, and a gift of hallucinated vision. Had these been controlled by a respect for impersonal reason, for common sense, for the objectivity of science, it would have been better for him. What his genius required, and what it sadly lacked, was a framework of accepted and traditional ideas that would have prevented him from indulging in a philosophy of his own and concentrated his attention upon the problems of the poet.

So says the famous Eliot, whose anxiety at the disruptions of the twentieth century and desire for the comforts of a received order made him, eventually, a staunch defender of reason, common sense, and objectivity. Of course, the most cursory reading of *The Waste Land* or "The Love Song of J. Alfred Prufrock" reveals immediately that the roots of his own poetry were in none of those things, but in deeply rooted traumas and wishes that found their way into the startling, unpredictable images and juxtapositions of these great poems.

Sensing that Eliot was more trustworthy as a poet than as a critic, especially of Blake's work, I was pleased to discover a much less famous but more sympathetic essay on Blake by the Quaker critic Harold C. Goddard. Rather than holding Blake to the standards of "impersonal reason" and "common sense"—as if those categories had served the human race, much less poets, as founts of unimpeachable wisdom—he regards Blake's lack of respect for "accepted and traditional ideas" as his great strength and celebrates his devotion to the imagination as engine of social change:

> Imagination cannot only cause that-which-was-not, to be; it can cause that-which-was, not to be. It is this double power to annihilate and create that makes imagination the sole instrument of genuine and lasting, in contrast with illusory and temporary, social change. . . . For art is the language of the imagination, the means by which the divine in man communicates with the divine in man, the coin that enables us to exchange LIFE. (35)

Goddard recognizes, with Hopper, that dismantling of received errors is as necessary as the creation of new insight. Elsewhere, he claims that Blake's scheme, the famous, difficult system he arduously worked out (so Blake claimed) lest he be "enslaved to another man's," addresses the key problem that Blake saw in the world, and which is symbolized in one of the key events of Blake's life: his forceful expulsion of a drunken soldier from his garden one evening. (Blake was tried on trumped-up charges of sedition following this incident, but found not guilty.) "There is a drunken soldier in the garden of the world at present," Goddard writes powerfully: surely the crucial issue of our day, as of Blake's, is how to contend with those who are both trained to violence and "drunken" enough with the power of violence to think that it actually solves problems.

According to Goddard, Blake's answer to this problem fuses imagination and action, desire and reason, at least within the visionary space of the poem. Blake's "fourfold vision," then, is a climb up a kind of Jacob's Ladder from darkness to vision. Single Vision is standard eyesight. Double Vision is metaphor—cf. the Tyger. The dynamic interplay of images is Threefold Vision, as in dreams. "Whoever has known imaginative love, whoever has created a work of art and felt inspired at the moment he conceived it has an inkling of Blake's state of threefold vision" (31). And Fourfold Vision is "dreaming (or loving, or imagining—they are three forms of the same thing) with such intensity that the dream obliterates daylight as daylight ordinarily obliterates the dream" (31). "If the two worlds remain at odds, if the ship of dreams is wrecked on the rocks of reality, we have at the weakest daydreaming, at the strongest hallucination or insanity. But if the two coalesce, as it were, if the ship sails the seas of reality successfully, we have fourfold vision" (31).

> I give you the end of a golden string,
> Only wind it into a ball,
> It will lead you in at Heaven's gate
> Built in Jerusalem's wall. (Blake 462)

Jerusalem, Goddard argues, "means the City of Perfect Liberty. In other words, it is not just individual, but social ecstasy and vision that Blake seeks. Put more men, more often, into a more elevated state of imagination, and everything else follows" (34).

This *is* a faith, if one of an unaccustomed sort. If Blake offers no action plan for practical political action, his vision is surprisingly pragmatic in its real-world implications, although (as G.K. Chesterton remarked of Christianity) it has mainly proven difficult and been left untried. An antinomianism that would transcend Law through the Imagination, that would bring Jerusalem into being by vision rather than by will? Difficult, surely. Yet this romantic rhetoric of Blake's, Goddard suggests, offers a way out of another problematic dualism: "Our forefathers believed in individual salvation. We believe in social salvation. Either without the other is futile, Blake believes. Indeed 'society' and 'the individual' are simply two more of those abstractions of the Reason that he abhorred. Like Heaven and Hell they must be 'married' before there can be creation" (34).

To walk with Blake and to see through his eyes, I might suggest, is to glimpse the "grain of the universe" of which John Howard Yoder speaks—and no less than Yoder, Blake believed and desired that grain to move toward justice and peace. As the image of "fourfold vision" suggests, however, we must not rush too quickly from Book to Ethics, from text to behavior (text written by bodies), without taking sufficient account of the passage through language and imagination without which no text can be written and no effective action can take place.

I had nearly finished this essay when I encountered John D. Cavuto's fine essay "On Being Clear About Faith." He argues eloquently and persuasively that although religious language and narratives need not—cannot—be regarded as providers of unmediated Truth, they still have much to offer as they move believers to act on the moral imperatives that they embody:

> What then *are* religious revelations ultimately about? They are centrally made up of important religious narratives that shape the lives of the faithful in that tradition; they are formative not informative. They don't reveal (or "report") secret bits of information to us—like the identity of Deep Throat—about the transactions of angels but they imaginatively embody a form of life. [...] Are they true? Yes. But we are thinking about their "truth" in the wrong way if we take them as supplying clear knowledge in a representational theory of truth. Their truth—and this is what I think *vera religio* comes down to—comes in the way of the fruitfulness of the form of life to which they give rise, which they both shape and embody.

Cavuto argues, in effect, for a poetic view of religious language, and like Blake, he insists that such a view is more, not less, practical than a rationalist or legalist approach. We need religion because it feeds our souls, and through the feeding of souls, we discover that living faith requires much more of us than assent to some set of abstract propositions. We can no more live fruitfully without well-cultivated inner lives than we can drive our cars for a decade without changing the oil or checking the battery. There *are* "ghosts in the house" of our beings, as David Miller argues, and if we fail to converse with them, they are likely to do all sorts of damage. Miller suggests that instead of ignoring, repressing, or seeking to bind these ghosts, we ought to "entertain" them, "as a host would entertain a guest" (158). If we allow the ghosts that inhabit the world, our texts, our selves, to speak openly, he suggests, they may have a great deal to teach us.

III.

The turn to theopoetics, if we choose to make it, takes us back to poetry, where communication with spirits of all sorts is ongoing. Mennonite poet Julia Spicher Kasdorf explores this practice memorably in her essay "When the Stranger Is an Angel," which considers both the biblical injunction to offer hospitality to strangers—who may be angels after all—and their potentially transformative power. Speaking of the story of Jacob wresting with the angel and a family story of a visiting hobo, Kasdorf muses startlingly on their implications:

> Perhaps this story—like my father's story—means that we possess a sacred power to make angels out of strangers when we are open to change. This can only happen when we leave the security of the hearth and go out to greet the stranger, when we sit with him and imagine his life, when we are able to question our certainties with him and be taught and changed by the encounter. (*The Body*, 35)

Kasdorf's poem "Bat Boy, Break a Leg" returns to this theme, interweaving two encounters with strangers and enacting just this sort of patient openness:

> The student with two studs in his nose
> and a dragon tattoo crawling from his collar,
>   who seems always ready to swoon
>   from bliss or despair, now flits
> At my office door. I will look at his poem
> drawn onto a music score and find nothing
>   to say about chance or HIV.

>   Only later I'll think to tell him
> the night before I left home, I slept
> sadly in our old house until a wing
>   touched my cheek, tenderly as a breeze.
>   I woke to black fluttering at my feet,
> and a mind fresh from the other side
> said *don't turn on the light, don't*
>   *Wake the man, don't scream or speak.*
>   *Go back to sleep.* The next morning
> I remembered that people upstate
> whack them with tennis rackets, that
>   the Chinese character for good luck
>   resembles the character for bat—
> both so unsettling and erratic—
> but it's bad luck to say good luck
>   in China, as on stage where they say
>   *Break a leg*, so delicate bats
> must be woven into silk brocade
> and glazed onto porcelain plates.
>   Next morning, I found a big-eared mouse
>   with leather folded over his shoulders
> hanging from claws stuck in a screen.
> All day, my work made me forget, but
>   then I'd remember, passing the window
>   where he slept, shaded under the eaves.
> He was fine. I was fine. Then at dusk,
> he was gone, suddenly. Pale boy dressed in black,
>   Maybe the best that can be said for any of us is that
>   once we were angelic enough to sleep with strangers.
> He touched my cheek. I opened the screen.
> He flew in his time. We did no harm.

Most notably, this poem not only tests and reaffirms nonviolence, but extends it to animals and other such strangers, without waking "the man" who can be expected to react with an aggressive defense of his home against the intruder. Making peace with bats? Shocking.

Many poems in Jean Janzen's fine new book, *Paper House,* also challenge and even contradict conventional religious thinking, even as they search for signs of holy presence. In the playful "Five Lessons on Piety" a blue jay "screeches his piety,/then steals the bagel from my plate," and "The old poet strums his guitar and sings/'O Piety, how close you lie to Heresy'" (27). The startling "Liminal" investigates the threshold between this world and the next:

> Sometimes it is the scent
> of peach, smooth and sweet
> as a newborn, or the newborn
>
> breathing in soft flutter.
> Or the river, relentless
> and disappearing.
>
> Nothing firm, like granite,
> which bars them entrance, yet
> having been born in fire
>
> could become fire again.
> Then is the doorway everywhere—
> grass, bread, your hand gesturing?
>
> Or language, your voice saying,
> "here it is," a place
> we can almost glimpse. (45)

My own recent poems have also often been investigations of crossings and openings between everyday life and the other realms, interior and exterior, that seem more and more palpable to me. Whatever the reason, I find myself drawn more and more to obscure and ambitious texts and authors, those unwilling to trust that the standard wisdom and common sense exhaust everything that we were meant to know and experience. Like Janzen's "Liminal," although without her admirable economy, "Damselfly" explores thresholds and possible openings into new life:

Damselfly

Beginnings have an irritating but essential fragility, and one that should be taken to heart.

–Teilhard de Chardin

Consider that ant swarm on the sidewalk, like spilled brown sugar, and the pale yellow leaves the hackberry casts free in a dry June, pressed to the parking lot.

The gray uneven two-by-fours of the picnic table, no place to set a cup half full or half empty.

A green grain head, waving from the corner the mower can't reach.

Elijah's cloak parting the waters, and Elisha: "Let me inherit a double-share of your spirit." And Elijah: "Your request is a difficult one."

And the bowl with the coiled serpent in its heart. And *This is my body*. And the stones of the creek, surfacing with the drought.

When spoken, the secret is no longer the secret. I am not good at secrets. The God I love speaks only in roars and whispers. The God I love only seems to play favorites.

At nine it is already humid, and the woods are dressed in their seven summer greens. All around me the machines are sorting and sifting, cutting and burning.

I wait a whole minute and a black damselfly crosses the creek and the world begins again and again.
And far away right here in town, the child wakes and rolls and stretches, not yet hungry. Wide-eyed, he waves and coos to bring the day into his blue-tinted room.

And there she is, smiling in the open door. (*Spoken* xi-xii)

One spark for my recent thinking has been poet Donald Revell's innovative prose book *Invisible Green*. Discussing poet Ronald Johnson's *Ark*, Revell quotes a passage from Thoreau's journal in which Thoreau drinks at a stream and imagines that he has drunk more than water: an arrowhead, or some ova, or perhaps seeds of thought. Thoreau muses that those who would drink at "running streams, the living waters" must be ready to "suckle monsters" with unpredictable results. Yet doing so is preferable to drinking from stagnant waters:

> Is there not such a thing as getting rid of the snake which you have swallowed when young, when thoughtless you stooped and drank at stagnant waters, which has worried you in your waking hours and your sleep ever since, and appropriated the life that was yours? (126)

Here, the key act is drinking from the fresh stream, rather than from the "stagnant waters" that conceal snakes. Revell offers this reading:

> Thoreau, and with Thoreau, Johnson, here describe practices prior to Religion, behaviors beyond Law. They were antinomians in the active, innocent sense. (Like Blake before, each propounded the vigor of unoriginal innocence, one whose unharming energies vivify, perhaps even maintain, the originating world-as-found.) (127)

This is the heretical sublime, or one of its faces: in such strange and disturbing stories that rise, strong and dangerous as snakes, from some deep hollow within, refusing to be neatly contained or explained, but demanding to be reckoned. These stories seem indeed to be "before" or outside religion, not to be contained by its names and categories. Indeed, I would claim, they are products of some "unoriginal innocence," which may be another name for imagination, whose strongest claim is that it emerges from the very ground of being and of Being, which sometimes, in some of its manifold attributes, we call God.

Works Cited

Bangs, Jeremy Dupuis, 2004, *Letters on Toleration: Dutch Aid to Persecuted Swiss and Palatine Mennonites 1615-1699*, Rockport, ME: Picton Press.

Blake, William, 1970, "*Jerusalem, Selected Poems and Prose,*" edited by Hazard Adams, New York: Holt, Rinehart and Winston.

Bly, Robert, 1986, *Selected Poems*, New York: Harper and Row.

Caputo, John D., "On Being Clear About Faith: A response to Stephen Williams," Books & Culture: A Christian Review. http://www.christianitytoday.com/bc/2006/novdec/18.40.html?start=1 (accessed August 11, 2009).

Carson, Anne, 1998, *Eros the Bittersweet*, Urbana-Champaign: University of Illinois, Dalkey Archive Press.

Eliot, Thomas Stearns, *The Sacred Wood*, London: Methune, [1920]; Bartleby.com, 1996. http://www.bartleby.com/200/ (accessed May 26, 2006).

Goddard, Harold, C., 1956, *Blake's Fourfold Vision*, Wallingford, PA: Pendle Hill.

Gundy, Jeff, 2007, *Spoken among the Trees*, Akron, OH: University of Akron Press.

Gundy, Jeff, 2005, *Walker in the Fog: On Mennonite Writing*, Telford, PA: Cascadia.

Heidegger, Martin, 1949, *Existence and Being*, translated and introduced by, Werner Brock, Chicago: Henry Regnery.

Heidegger, Martin, 1971, *Poetry, Language, Thought*, translated by Albert Hofstadter, New York: Harper.

Hopper, Stanley Romaine, 1992, *The Way of Transfiguration: Religious Imagination as Theopoiesis*, edited by R. Melvin Keiser and Tony Stoneburner, Louisville, KY: Westminster.

Kasdorf, Julia, Bat Boy, Break a Leg, *Shenandoah* 51.4 (Winter 2001).

Kaufman, Gordon, 2004, *In the Beginning... Creativity*, Minneapolis: Fortress.

Klassen, Peter J., 2009, *Mennonites in Early Modern Poland and Prussia*, Baltimore: Johns Hopkins University Press.

Kaplan, Benjamin J., 2007, *Divided by Faith: Religious Conflict and the Practice of Toleration in Early Modern Europe*, Cambridge: Harvard University Press.

Miller, David L., 1989, *Hells & Holy Ghosts: A Theopoetics of Christian Belief*, Nashville: Abindgon Press.

Yoder, John Howard, 1992, *Body Politics: Five Practices of the Christian Community Before the Watching World*, Scottdale, PA: Herald Press.

Yoder, John Howard, 1984, *The Priestly Kingdom: Social Ethics as Gospel*, Notre Dame, IN: University of Notre Dame Press.

Notes

1. For recent explorations of the struggle to achieve religious tolerance in Europe, see Bangs, Kaplan, and Klassen.
2. Cf. the critique of "binary dualisms" by Derrida, Foucault, and other postmodern theorists, almost two centuries later.

THEOPOETICS
Si(g)ns of Copulation

Crystal Downing

What theology needs is more copulation. And postmodern theopoetics may well provide it.

The word copulation, of course, denotes coupling: the bringing together and/or union of two things. The related words "copula" and "copulative" are grammatical terms, used to describe the linking of elements in a sentence. How unfortunate, then, that the fertile term *copulation* has been reduced in meaning, often with the limited connotation of animal(istic) sex.

In the sixteenth century, however, copulation was still robust, the word used not only for sex and grammar, but also for theology. The *OED* exemplifies the word's breadth with an illustration from 1548: "The wonderful copulation of the sayed nature vnto ours by his incarnation." The dictionary's example from 1623 implies that the copulation of divine and human in the Christ-event elicits copulation on the part of Christ's followers: "The copulation of a living faith and obedience together."

In this essay, I will argue that theopoetics, if truly postmodern, returns us to the copulation of living faith and obedience—if even in different terms than dreamt of in the philosophy of 1623, a year tremendously significant to any *authentic* lover of poetics. For 1623 is the publication date of the First Folio of Shakespeare's works.

My allusion to this definitive text of Western poetics, wherein appears "There are more things in heaven and earth, Horatio,/Than are dreamt of in your philosophy," has a purpose. There is, as it were, method to my madness. For by aligning the "authentic" with the First Folio, I intentionally signal a failure of copulation. I have overpowered theology with a narrow definition of poetics, assuming that knowledge of practitioners in my discipline, literary studies, instantiates authenticity.

Something similar tempts theologians drawn to theopoetics: by ignoring the copulation signaled by the term theopoetics—the coupling of Greek roots for *god* and *to make*—some reduce theology to poetical practices. In contrast, I will encourage the copulation inherent to postmodern theopoetics, distinguishing it from the onanism of theopoetics in a modernist style. I will then illustrate postmodern theopoetics with the creativity of Dorothy L. Sayers, a theopoet ahead of her time.

Modernist versus postmodern poetic practices

My distinction between modernist and postmodern theopoetics parallels the difference between high modernist and postmodern attitudes about poetry. Central to the distinction is the concept of autonomy. High modernism was spawned by the copulation of Cartesian rationalism and Lockean empiricism in the philosophy of Immanuel Kant, who defined enlightenment as "the courage to use your own intelligence." As Stanley Grenz once put it, Kant "believed that the burden of discovering truth is ultimately a private matter, that the knowing process is fundamentally a relationship between the autonomous knowing self and the world waiting to be known."[1]

While Kant privileged reason as the engine driving the autonomous knowing self, the 19th century Romantic poets elevated imagination as the primary power energizing the autonomous perceiver. By the 20th century, autonomy was associated with the poetic artifact itself. In the 1950s, novelist E. M. Forster asserted that a true poem "points to nothing but itself," while literary critic Northrop Fry proclaimed the importance "of producing a structure of words for its own sake," calling such a structure "autonomous."[2]

Even poetic style was meant to be autonomous, as implied by the 20th century neologism "free verse." Entering the English language in 1908, *free verse* was a translation of the French *vers libre,* first used in 1902 (*OED*). Modernist advocates of free verse eschewed conventional forms like the sonnet or the sestina, refusing to follow any rhyme scheme or pre-established rhythm whatsoever. Ezra Pound, whose 1914 anthology *Des Imagistes* became the cynosure of the new poetics, preached a principle that became the creed of high modernism: "Make It New!" By celebrating free verse as free from the prejudice of traditional styles, Pound illustrates Gadamer's famous aphorism about modernism: "the prejudice against prejudice." Dominating poetics for much of the twentieth century, "Make It New" became the modernist tradition against tradition.

Postmodernism, of course, problematized this tradition. Establishing that all practices—whether poetic, scientific, historical, political, or theological—are embedded in and molded by the prejudices of discourse, postmodern theorists subverted the autonomy of make-it-newism with language about deconstruction (Derrida), power (Foucault), metanarratives (Lyotard), the law of the father (Lacan), rhizomes (Deleuze and Guattari), hybridity (Bhaba), performativity (Butler), and the contingency of our vocabularies (Rorty).

Developing alongside these postmodern paradigms was a literary movement called "The New Formalism": a movement that returned poetics to tradition. In 1968, the year that Roland Barthes published "The Death of the Author" and Foucault published "What Is an Author?"—both of which challenged the modernist mystification of autonomy—poet Lewis Turco published *The Book of Forms: A Handbook of Poetics*. Generating as much disgust among modernists as did Barthes and Foucault, Turco resurrected rhyme and meter as well as traditional poetic forms like the highly complex villanelle and sestina.

Modernist versus postmodern theopoetics

The division within 20th century poetics between modernist autonomy and postmodern embeddedness is mirrored in 21st century theopoetics. Some practitioners, manifesting a prejudice against prejudice, perpetuate the tradition against tradition as they seek to Make God New. For them, any poem, song, or dance becomes theological if it is freshly created—or received—with spiritual intent and/or openness to mystery. Like free verse, theopoetics thus becomes an autonomous work of theology.

Significantly, high modernists sanctified free verse as having divine status, as when E. M. Forster proclaimed "A poem is absolute. . . . it is eternal and indestructible." Literary critic I. A. Richards went so far as to say that poetry is "capable of saving us; it is a perfectly possible means of overcoming chaos": theopoetics in a modernist key.[3]

In contrast, theopoetics fully informed by postmodern theory refuses to mystify the making-new—just as it refuses to mystify the ancient-made. Recognizing that no human has unmediated access to absolute truth, genuinely postmodern theopoets—similar to New Formalists—embrace tradition, accepting their indebtedness to ancient forms even as they work to re-form them. Rather than the arrogant (and naïve) autonomy of the make-it-new creed, postmodern theopoetics celebrates the copulation of past and present, tradition and change, theo and poetics.

Postmodern copulation: Richard Rorty and tradition(ing)

The postmodern theopoet incarnates what Richard Rorty calls "the vanguard of the species": the "strong poet."[4] In *Contingency, Irony, and Solidarity*, Rorty argues for discursive determinism, wherein a society's perceptions and practices are regulated by the language its members speak—a vocabulary that is entirely arbitrary, without any grounding in or direct access to truth. Strong poets, however, recognizing the contingency of their society's vocabulary, work to ironize it, drawing attention to its insufficiencies and its regulatory powers by creating metaphors that capture human experience in new ways. Copulating linguistic determinism with free will, then, strong poets squeeze the language constitutive of their own knowledge into unusual molds, creating forms that reflect old and new at once.

Church historian Dale T. Irvin illustrated the strong poet when he coined the term "traditioning," squeezing a static noun—tradition—into the mold of a dynamic gerund: tradition*ing*. By signaling a "dialogical relationship between present and past," the coinage avoids mystifying either tradition or anti-tradition: "Both those who hold to the detraditionalization thesis and those who support the notion of traditions being unchanging and unchangeably given, fail to recognize the dynamic process of rejuvenation and re-creation that has taken place across the centuries and continues today to give traditions ongoing life."[5] Copulating past and present, stasis and change, Irvin's theopoetic invention challenges fundamentalists on both the right and left: from traditionalists who revile change to modernists who revile tradition.

Like postmodern theopoetics, traditioning is a "constructive activity," expressing ancient truths in new ways, making them relevant to and for contemporary culture.[6] However, as with any change, there is always a risk to traditioning, as indicated by the etymology of the word. Coming from the Latin *traditio*, the word *tradition* means "the 'handing over'" and contains connotations of betrayal, as in the related words "traitor" and "traduce." When one generation "hands over" a tradition to another, the earlier group no longer has control of it, allowing for the possibility of change to and hence betrayal of ancient interpretations.

The Greek word for "handing over"— *paradidomi*—is used in the Christian Scriptures to signal radically different events. Not surprisingly, it describes the actions of Judas and Pilate as they hand over Jesus to his murderers. But, as Irvin notes, "the same verb (or its cognates) names the process of passing on authentic memory of Jesus Christ, and hence of Christian identity from one group of persons or one generation to another."[7] These two senses come together in one of the most familiar passages in the New Testament. Providing instructions for the Lord's Supper, Paul writes to the Corinthians, "For I received from the Lord what I also handed on [*paredoka*] to you, that the Lord Jesus on the night when he was betrayed [*paredideto*] took a loaf of bread, and when he had given thanks, he broke it and said, 'This is my body that is for you. Do this in remembrance of me'" (I Cor 11: 23-24). Paul's pun, whether intentional or not, implies that the tradition he is handing over is meaningful not *in spite of* but because of what happened after the supper in the upper room: Jesus was handed over to his enemies.

The etymological connection between *tradition* and *betrayal* leads Irvin to an interesting conclusion:

> In every act of authentic traditioning there remains something of an act of treason, otherwise it would not be an authentic act of handing over, of change. Without a bit of treason performed in the act of handing over, the tradition remains inseparably bound to the world in which it was formed, hence not only irrelevant but incomprehensible.[8]

Christian playwright Dorothy L. Sayers (1893-1957) provides a perfect illustration of Irvin's point: in 1941 she was quite literally accused of treason for her theopoetic efforts.[9]

The treason of Dorothy L. Sayers

In 1940, the British Broadcasting Corporation (BBC) asked Sayers—by then a famous detective fiction novelist—to write a series of twelve radio plays about the life of Jesus. Quite earnest in her commitment to both *theo* and *poetics*, Sayers agreed to the project, deciding to "hand over"—in both senses—the ancient story of Christ's bodily resurrection. In December of 1941, the BBC held a press conference in which Sayers read passages from her finished work. Journalists pounced on her abnormal language, embellishing the fact that Sayers put slang—worse, American slang (!)—into disciples' mouths. As one headline put it, "BBC Life of Christ Play in U.S. Slang."

In *Philosophy and the Mirror of Nature*, Rorty distinguishes between "abnormal" and "normal" language, explaining that the abnormal occurs when someone sets aside "an agreed-upon set of conventions."[10] So when Sayers set aside the normal "stained-glass-window decorum with which the tale [of Jesus] is usually presented to us," as she puts it in her introduction to the printed play-cycle,[11] she fulfilled Rorty's sense of the strong poet: "The line between weakness and strength is . . . the line between using language which is familiar and universal and producing language which, though initially unfamiliar and idiosyncratic, somehow makes tangible the blind impress all one's behavings bear."[12]

Unfortunately, when it comes to religion and politics, many people, on both the right and the left, are blind to the impress of discourse on their behavior. They can assess someone's *correctness*—whether political or religious—only by hearing "language which is familiar." Sayers's abnormal language therefore created a national scandal. Organizations like The Protestant Truth Society and The Lord's Day Observance Society mounted a letter-writing campaign, petitioning Winston Churchill and the Archbishop of Canterbury to ban the broadcasts. In the protesters' minds, Sayers's theopoetic re-scripting of the Bible was a betrayal of the "Authorized Version" of truth. One critic went so far as to align Sayers's "handing over" with current events of World War II. Suggesting that Singapore fell to the Axis powers because of the BBC broadcast, he demanded that the plays be taken off the air "before a like fate came to Australia."[13] Sayers's poetic rendering of the biblical text was, for him, treasonous. Her fertile "copulation of a living faith and obedience together" was adulterous.

Fortunately, the BBC resisted tremendous pressure to cancel the radio productions—and certainly benefited from the free advertising. Sayers's plays were broadcast as scheduled, thousands of people tuning in precisely because of the scandal. What they got was theopoetics. Though Sayers received numerous "abusive anonymous letters"—one addressing her "You nasty old sour-puss"[14]—she also heard from scores of listeners who testified that, for the first time in their lives, the Bible made sense to them, that they finally understood how following Jesus could be relevant to regular slang-slinging, working-class individuals like themselves.[15]

The handing over of Judas

Accusations of treason generated by Sayers's radio plays were anticipated, ironically enough, by one of her cycle's key characters. In the eighth play, Sayers establishes that the fatal flaw of Judas was his insensitivity to theopoetics. As she notes in the introduction to the published cycle, "simple-minded people" who regard Judas as a "creeping, crawling, patently worthless villain," end up "cast[ing] too grave a slur upon the brains or the character of Jesus."[16] In other words, radical vilification of Judas implies that Jesus was either too naive to recognize his follower's evil intentions, or else too manipulative (using an evil man to achieve his purposes) to warrant our respect.

Sayers therefore makes Judas "the most intelligent of all the disciples," fully understanding and intensely devoted to his Lord's sacrificial mission.[17] Grasping the significance of Jesus better than any other disciple, Judas's strength, however, becomes his greatest weakness: his passionate commitment to Christ turns into certitude about his ability to understand the word of God. He becomes so committed to *his own interpretation* of sacred truth that he accuses Jesus of treason when the latter acts differently than Judas anticipated.

Sayers's Judas loses confidence in Jesus during the Triumphal Entry. Seeing jubilant crowds wave palm branches and shout "Hosanna" as Jesus rides an ass into Jerusalem, Judas comes to the conclusion that his one-time Lord has "sold himself" to a political revolution. Out of commitment to "the truth," then, Judas willingly betrays his leader, telling Caiaphas, "Jesus is corrupt to the bone. [. . .] I believed in his pretensions. I supported his claim. [. . .] I sincerely thought he had sufficient character to resist temptation. I suppose I was a fool to trust him."[18]

Ironically, the actions that Judas regarded as signs of corruption actually prove the purity of Christ's purposes. In Sayers's fictionalized scenario, Judas does not know that, earlier in the day, Jesus had received a note from "Baruch the Zealot," stating,

> In the stable of Zimri, at the going-up into the City, is a war-horse saddled and ready. Set yourself upon him, and you shall ride into Jerusalem with a thousand spears behind you. But if you refuse, then take the ass's colt that is tied at the vineyard door, and Baruch will bide his time till a bolder Messiah come. (203)

By choosing the ass's colt, then, Jesus was refusing to instigate a political revolution. His decision to follow a God of peace rather than a lord of war leads to the cross rather than a coup, to resurrection rather than insurrection.

In her theopoetic reconstruction of biblical events, then, Sayers honors tradition even while establishing that arrogant certitude about truth betrays Jesus. Confident that he understood the will of God, Judas rejected the copulation of *theo* and *poetics* in Christ.

Copulating Marys

Sayers makes such copulation explicit in her treatment of the iconic figure who, within the Roman Catholic tradition, resists all copulation: the Virgin Mary. As though alluding to the *OED*'s 1548 example—"The wonderful copulation of the sayed nature vnto ours by his incarnation"—Sayers calls Mary "fact" and God "truth," asserting that literal body (fact) and figurative meaning (truth) were united through the incarnation. In the eleventh radio-play, the Virgin states, "I, Mary, am the fact; God is the truth; but Jesus is fact and truth—he is reality. You cannot see the immortal truth till it is born in the flesh of the fact" (289). This last sentence provides a motivation for theopoetic copulation: immortal truth, like the transcendental signified, is always already inaccessible to mortal flesh. Truth, conceived through tradition, must be born in the flesh—either through praxis or poetics: the practice of love or the making of beauty. And Sayers implies that the copulation of truth and fact in the Virgin's womb created both. Witnessing the harrowing events on the Via Dolorosa, the Virgin moans, "This is the worst thing; to conceive beauty in your heart and bring it forth into the world, and then to stand by helpless and watch it suffer" as it embodies an act of love (289).

Furthermore, Sayers establishes that the Virgin can reach the site of that act—the cross—only by way of beauty. When Roman soldiers prevent the Madonna, John, and Mary Magdalen from approaching the dying Jesus, the character traditionally aligned with sexual copulation creates art.[19] Removing her veil and unpinning her red hair, Magdala seeks access to Christ by singing and dancing for soldiers she had once entertained more salaciously: "By the feet that danced for you, by the voice that sang for you, by the beauty that delighted you—Marcellus, let me pass!" Resisting her overtures, Marcellus dismisses any connection between beauty and Jesus: "Beauty! that's for living men. What is this dying gallows bird to you?" (298). Magdala, however, had already provided an answer in the previous scene. Seeing Jesus bloodied by torture, she describes him in terms of beauty: "O swift feet! O strong hands! O face that was the beauty of Israel! Where are the lips that laughed away our sorrow? Where is the voice that called back Lazarus from the grave?" (291-2). The erotic tinge of Magdala's words reflects Sayers's point: that Magdala renounces a life of superficial sexual copulation in recognition of the far more provocative beauty of copulation in Christ: "the copulation of a living faith and obedience together." Moved by this beauty, Magdala continues performing for Roman soldiers, until the beauty of her art opens a passageway to Jesus—not only for herself but also for those accompanying her.

So also the beauty of Sayers's art created a passageway to Jesus for hundreds of BBC listeners who had once regarded Christian tradition with indifference if not disdain. They clearly valued Sayers's imaginative reconstruction of the Christ-event, her copulation of *theo* and *poetics*, of truth and fact. As Sayers puts it in a 1942 lecture, the "function of imaginative speech is not to prove, but to create—to discover new similarities and to arrange them to form new unities."[20]

Those traditionalists who reviled her imaginative speech therefore mimicked her Caiaphas, who, in the eleventh play, states, "It is the duty of statesmen to destroy the madness which we call imagination. It is dangerous. It breeds dissension. Peace, order, security—that is Rome's offer—at Rome's price" (296-97). The theopoet, in contrast, refuses hegemonic offers of order and security, of certitude and stability.

Significantly, Sayers aligns Caiaphas with the hegemonic forces of her own day. In her introduction to the published version of the plays, *The Man Born to Be King,* Sayers writes, "Caiaphas was the ecclesiastical politician, appointed, like one of Hitler's bishops, by a heathen government, expressly that he might collaborate with the New Order and see that the Church toed the line drawn by the State; we have seen something of Caiaphas lately" (7). Sayers's reference to the New Order suggests her own suspicions about modernist make-it-newism, Hitler providing an extreme example. Aware of the man who coined "Make It New" (the love of her life was published in *Des Imagistes*), Sayers would not have been surprised to discover that Ezra Pound became an emphatic supporter of Mussolini.

In contrast, Sayers so renounced certitude that she turned down an honorary doctorate in divinity with the words, "I am never quite sure whether I really am [a Christian], or whether I have only fallen in love with an intellectual pattern."[21] Ironically, some biographers suggest that Sayers turned down the honor because of si(g)ns of copulation in her body. In 1924, as the result of an extra-marital affair, Sayers gave birth to a son, whom she supported her entire life but whose existence she hid from all friends and family except the cousin who raised the boy for her. Her illicit copulation, biographers argue, made Sayers feel unworthy of a doctorate in divinity.[22]

I, however, believe that copulation of another sort engendered Sayers's resistance to the doctorate. Like another prophet of theopoetics, Sayers had suspicions about the copula.

Copulating Dorothy Sayers and Jacques Derrida

Born just as Sayers was achieving financial independence as a best-selling author, Jacques Derrida, that pre-eminent prophet of postmodern theopoetics, also combated certitude through copulation. He did so by questioning copulative grammar, problematizing the copula—the to-be verb—itself. By putting an X over the copula "is" in some of his early writings, Derrida subverted the universalizing certitude of the to-be verb as it couples a subject with a predicate.[23]

For example, if I were to proclaim "killing is wrong," someone might protest, "Well, it depends on the context. What about killing perpetrators of genocide? What about killing in self-defense? What about killing chickens for food? What about killing a news story that has proven inaccurate?" Such questions demonstrate that my "is," the copula of my sentence, does not capture the complete truth. Indeed, the word "killing," as Saussure has taught us, is inevitably embedded in larger systems of signification. In response to these protests, then, I could follow the lead of Derrida by putting an "X" over my "to be" verb:

Killing i̶s̶ wrong

By doing so, I put my copula "under erasure."[24] In other words, I do not suddenly reverse myself by saying "Killing is not wrong." Instead, I hold onto my belief—killing is wrong—even as I signal, with an X, that changes in context qualify my belief. And, of course, changes in culture over time count as changes in context.

Thus, just as Sayers qualified her Christianity by proclaiming "I am never quite sure whether I really am one," Derrida qualified his atheism by proclaiming "I rightly pass for an atheist."[25] Rather than stating "I *am* an atheist," he avoids the "to be" verb altogether. By using the word "pass" rather than a copula, Derrida implies that signs of atheism in his life are only on the surface—as when a light-skinned African-American "passes" as a Caucasian. However, at the same time, his word "rightly" implies that his signs of atheism may be accurate. Derrida thus asserts his inclination toward atheism while also putting it under erasure, indicating that he is open to something atheists consider impossible: God.[26]

Putting the copula under erasure signals "openness toward the other": the fundamental ethic of postmodernism and hence of postmodern theopoetics.[27] Unfortunately, many of Derrida's followers practiced theopoetics of the modernist kind. As postmodern theologian Mark C. Taylor notes in his obituary, "Betraying Mr. Derrida's insights by creating a culture of political correctness, his self-styled supporters fueled the culture wars that have been raging for more than two decades and continue to frame political debate." In contrast, Derrida argued that "it is necessary to recognize the unavoidable limitations and inherent contradictions in the ideas and norms that guide our actions, and do so in a way that keeps them open to constant questioning and continual revision."[28]

For Dorothy Sayers, Church dogma offers the ideas and norms that guide Christian actions—ideas and norms that she questioned and revised through the poetics of theater. As she emphatically asserted in her essay "The Dogma Is the Drama,"

> Let us, in Heaven's name, drag out the Divine Drama from under the dreadful accumulation of slipshod thinking and trashy sentiment heaped upon it, and set it on an open stage to startle the world into some sort of vigorous reaction. If the pious are the first to be shocked, so much the worse for the pious—others will enter the Kingdom of Heaven before them.[29]

Sayers recognized that dogma, like drama, becomes rote when participants reiterate their scripts to the point of unthinking reiteration of diction and unreflective miming of gestures. Group solidarity can solidify dogma into dogmatism, such that protecting the script becomes an end in itself.

Sayers advocated, instead, "creative mind," going so far as to argue that humans are most godlike when they create. Inspired by the tradition of the *imago Dei*, Sayers wrote *The Mind of the Maker* in 1940 as an exploration of what it means to be created in the image of God (Genesis 1:27). She quotes from Nicholas Berdyaev's *The Destiny of Man* (1931) to summarize her views:

> God created man in his own image and likeness, i.e., made him a creator too, calling him to free spontaneous activity and not to formal obedience to His power. Free creativeness is the creature's answer to the great call of its creator.[30]

Berdyaev's words, once rid of gender exclusivity, might help theorize a postmodern theopoetic, in which the "creative act," as Sayers puts it, offers "a kind of illumination upon the variety and inconclusiveness of the world about us."[31]

It is because of this inconclusiveness that Sayers saw the need to copulate theo, as conceptualized in traditional dogma, with poetics: "Poets create, we may say, by building up new images, new intellectual concepts, new worlds, if you like, to form new consistent wholes, new unities out of diversity."[32] Practicing what she preaches, Sayers rewrote that familiar statement of Jesus, "In my father's house are many mansions" (John 14:2), to emphasize the "building up" of new images. In *Man Born to Be King*, she has Jesus tell his disciples, "There are many inns on the road to my Father's house. I am going ahead to prepare the lodgings for you. You will always find me there to welcome you, so that at each stage we shall be together."[33] Theopoets, then, might be conceptualized as architects and carpenters constructing the many inns on the road to God.

Like Rorty's strong poet, theopoets develop new metaphors when the old ones become (to quote from the First Folio) "stale, flat, and unprofitable." Significantly, the character who mouthed these words, Hamlet, famously struggled with copulation, from exhorting his mother to stop copulating with King Claudius to asking that important question: "To be or not to be."

Sayers, from the right, like Derrida from the left, might answer "the question" by substituting *and* for Hamlet's *or*, thus copulating *to be* and *not to be*. Putting the copula under erasure in this way, they would unite "is" with "is not"—as when we copulate the everlasting "is" of *theo* with the reconstructive "is not" of *poetics*.

Notes

1. Immanuel Kant, "What Is Enlightenment?" in *The Philosophy of Kant*, ed. Karl J. Friedrich (New York: Modern Library, 1993), p. 145. Stanley Grenz, *A Primer on Postmodernism* (Grand Rapids, MI: Eerdmans, 1996), p. 80.
2. E. M. Forster, *Two Cheers for Democracy* (New York: Harcourt, 1951), p. 82; Northrop Frye, *Anatomy of Criticism: Four Essays* (Princeton, NJ: Princeton University Press, 1957), p. 74.
3. Forster, p. 82; I. A. Richards, *Science and Poetry* (New York: Norton, 1921), p. 95.
4. Richard Rorty, *Contingency, Irony, Solidarity* (Cambridge: Cambridge University Press, 1989), p. 20, 53. Rorty borrows the term "strong poet" from literary critic Harold Bloom.
5. Dale T. Irvin, *Christian Histories, Christian Traditioning: Rendering Accounts* (Maryknool, NY: Orbis, 1998), pp. 14, 9.
6. Ibid., p. 29.
7. Ibid., p. 40. Irvin refers his readers to Matt 26:25, Mark 14:21, Luke 22:21, Acts 3:13 and 6:14, and 2 Peter 2:21 for cognates of paradidomi.

8. Ibid., p. 41.

9. For an extended discussion of Sayers's traditioning, see my book *Writing Performances: The Stages of Dorothy L. Sayers* (New York: Palgrave Macmillan, 2004), especially Chapter Five. I insert several sentences from my book in what follows.

10. Richard Rorty, *Philosophy and the Mirror of Nature* (Princeton, NJ: Princeton University Press, 1979), p. 320.

11. Dorothy L. Sayers, *The Man Born to Be King: A Play-Cycle on the Life of our Lord and Saviour Jesus Christ* (Grand Rapids, MI: Eerdmans, 1979), p. 6.

12. Rorty, *Contingency*, pp. 28-29.

13. James W. Welch, "Forward," *The Man Born to Be King*, by Dorothy L. Sayers (London: Gollancz, 1946), p. 15.

14. *The Letters of Dorothy L. Sayers, 1937 to 1943: From Novelist to Playwright*, ed. Barbara Reynolds (New York: St. Martins, 1997), pp. 375, 377.

15. Listeners also benefited from the professionalism of the production. As I note elsewhere, "the producer was the brilliant Val Gielgud, brother of the famous actor Sir John Gielgud; Mary Magdalen was played by a young Hermione Gingold, perhaps best known for her superb role as the priggish mayor's wife in the classic film *The Music Man* (1962); and the music was composed by Benjamin Britten (whom Sayers called an "ASS"—but that is a different story)." See Crystal Downing, "The Bible as Babel: The Suspicions of Dorothy L. Sayers," in *From Around the Globe: Secular Authors and Biblical Perspectives*, ed. Seodial Frank H. Deena and Karoline Szatek (New York: University Press of America, 2007), p. 13.

16. Sayers, *Man Born to Be King*, p. 15.

17. Ibid., p. 52.

18. Ibid., p. 220.

19. In her introduction to the published cycle, Sayers explains that she coalesces Mary Magdalen with Mary of Bethany and the sinner of Luke 7. She justifies the gesture by copulating tradition with the needs of art: "This identification is, of course, traditional, and is sanctioned by the authority of St. Augustine of Hippo and Pope Gregory the Great. . . . The number of persons who flit, unheralded and unpursued, through the pages of the Gospel is enormous; and every legitimate opportunity was taken of tightening up the dramatic construction and avoiding the unnecessary multiplication of characters." *Man Born*, p. 16.

20. Dorothy L. Sayers, "Creative Mind," *The Whimsical Christian: 18 Essays by Dorothy L. Sayers* (New York: Macmillan, 1978), p. 109.

21. *The Letters of Dorothy L. Sayers*, p. 429.

22. This is most especially pronounced in James Brabazon, *Dorothy L. Sayers: A Biography* (New York: Scribner's, 1981). For a discussion of the post-structuralist implications of this, and other, biographies about Sayers, see chapter one of my *Writing Performances*.

23. Following the practice of Heidegger, Derrida put the copula under erasure to indicate the inability of *any* language to fully capture truth, to deliver a "metaphysics of presence." For an example of "X-ing" out the copula, see Jacques Derrida, *Of Grammatology*, trans. Gayatri Chakravorty Spivak (Baltimore: Johns Hopkins University Press, 1974), p. 44. Derrida grapples with philosophical implications of the copula in his 1971 essay "The Supplement of Copula: Philosophy before Linguistics," republished in Jacques Derrida, *Margins of Philosophy*, trans. Alan Bass (Chicago: University of Chicago Press, 1982), pp. 175-205.

24. Jacques Derrida, *Of Grammatology*, p. 60.
25. Jacques Derrida, "Circumfession," in *Jacques Derrida*, ed. Jacques Derrida and Geoffrey Bennington (Chicago: University of Chicago Press, 1993), p. 155.
26. For a helpful discussion of the theological implications of Derrida's "impossible," see Richard Kearney, "Deconstruction, God, and the Possible," in *Derrida and Religion: Other Testaments,* ed. Yvonne Sherwood and Kevin Hart (New York: Routledge, 2005), pp. 297-307.
27. Qtd. in "Dialogue with Jacques Derrida," in *Dialogues with Contemporary Continental Thinkers: The Phenomenological Heritage*, ed. Richard Kearney (Manchester, UK: Manchester University Press, 1984), 124.
28. Mark C. Taylor, "What Derrida Really Meant," *NY Times*, 14 October 2004, A29.
29. Sayers, "The Dogma Is the Drama," in *Creed or Chaos?* (Manchester, NH: Sophia Institute, 1974), p. 24.
30. Qtd. in Sayers, *The Mind of the Maker* (San Francisco: Harper Collins, 1941), p. 61.
31. Sayers, *The Mind of the Maker*, p. 52.
32. Sayers, "Creative Mind," p. 99.
33. Sayers, *Man Born to Be King*, p. 241.

KAVVANAH
The Poetry of Blessing and the Blessing of Poetry

David Harris Ebenbach

> It is Good to give thanks.
> Why? Does God need our praise?
> No.
> We do.
> *Rabbi Rami M. Shapiro*[1]

A couple of years ago I spent the second day of Rosh Hashanah, the Jewish new year, in an arboretum, alternately wandering under the trees and stopping to sit down with my prayerbook. Because it was the second day, I was already steeped in the power of the holiday, the themes of renewal, of memory and self-examination. For their part, the woods were readying themselves for fall—coloring in places, some leaves underfoot—and seemed to be having an experience parallel to mine. The world seemed alive with the opportunity for revelation. At one point, in a clearing, I was overcome with feeling, and what rose up in me was a kind of blessing—but, because I'm a writer, that blessing naturally took the form of a developing poem, one that I would later finish and entitle "Rosh Hashanah"[2]:

> Sun pours into the clearing
> through the forest's broken roof
> and the gnat
> as it wanders

becomes the movement of light—
some wavering piece of the above
here among us
as light—
a flare released by an unsteady hand
in the reach of the unsteady heart

What I was seeing, what I was feeling, was too powerful to ignore. I had to say something—and the poem was the way I had to say it.

There is a Jewish tradition of reciting a hundred blessings per day, a custom that requires you to offer up a virtually constant stream of thankfulness. Everything the devout person consumes, uses, sees; everywhere the devout person goes; everyone the devout person meets—all of this is supposed to receive focused, holy attention and intention—*kavvanah*, in Hebrew.[3] There are therefore specific blessings designed for just about everything: eating bread; eating fruit from trees or fruit that grows in the soil; witnessing an ocean, a rainbow, a shooting star; meeting a wise person; smelling spices; hearing good news; hearing bad news. The lesson is clear: we are supposed to find sacredness in every aspect of life.

When put like that, we can see that this isn't solely a Jewish idea; for one thing, it's also always been the credo of the poet, the person who finds beauty and meaning just about anywhere. In the words of Marge Piercy, "To be a poet is to open your eyes to everything around you."[4] Former United States Poet Laureate Robert Pinsky once said,

> There's a process of the human imagination's taking in its surroundings and discovering how to make art of them. What could be more unpromising than a steel oil drum? Smells bad, gets rusty, it's not attractive. But people took the steel oil drum and made music from it—a new *kind* of music....If there's something in your experience that moves you but seems without poetry, your challenge is to make it poetic.[5]

And so the poet's calling is the same as the calling of ancient Jewish tradition—as Piercy would have it in the title of one of her books, it's *the art of blessing the day*.[6]

But *why* bless? What's the point? If it's true that all things contain some reflection of the divine, some aspect of holiness, do they really need our recognition, our acknowledgment? Wasn't that clearing in the arboretum already beautiful and sacred before the poem started to come to me? When we start with the traditional words *Baruch atah adonai*—blessed are you, God—it raises the question: is this something that God really needs to hear? Isn't God, and God's creation, already plenty sacred without us having to say so?

Rabbi Teutsch, in the Reconstructionist Jewish prayerbook for Shabbat (the Sabbath), asks, "For whom do we recite blessings? If God is beyond blessing, then we must be reciting them for ourselves."[7] This is quite an idea—we are talking to God, but we are doing so, on some level, not for God but for *ourselves*. To give this kind of attention, whether to a rainbow or someone wise or a simple piece of bread, can be a powerful experience for us because "each *berahah* [blessing] urges us to avoid taking the world for granted. Each contains a vision of the creative or redemptive power in the world."[8] Similarly, according to Marcia Falk, "The poem keeps the world in front of the mind."[9] This vision is itself a gift—to ourselves, and, as we'll see, to others around us as well.

One thing that vision does is allow us to partake, in some measure, of the divine. Poet Allen Afterman said, "Recognition is the power to perceive the eternal in a person; the seeing through to the root of his soul. In this way, one is seeing him, as far as one is able, as God sees him."[10] By approaching the world with the *kavvanah* to bless, we become divine ourselves. This makes sense—in this moment we are creators ourselves, turning, in Teutsch's words, "ordinary things into gifts."[11] Nothing *is* ordinary, of course, but our careless perception might think otherwise without the focus, the *kavvanah*, required of us. *With* that *kavvanah*, we can create gifts—perhaps even poems. We can make holiness where there was none (in our limited eyes, anyway) before the blessing. We can understand the beauty of creation from within.

The obvious protest to all this is that not everything in creation *is* beautiful—what about natural disasters, disease, violence, human cruelty? Some things are ugly or horrifying or tragic. What do we do with things that seem worse than ordinary? Is it really incumbent on us to turn them into gifts?

Well, when Pinsky was talking about that oil drum, he didn't say it was boring—he said it "smells bad, gets rusty, it's not attractive." Nonetheless, his process leads from that apparent ugliness to something beautiful—the music of the steel drum band. Similarly, the traditional Jewish blessing upon seeing a rainbow—"Blessed are you, God, sovereign over the universe, who remembers the covenant [to never again flood the earth], remains faithful to it, and fulfills its word"—allows us to focus on the beautiful consequence of an uncomfortable or maybe even frightening rain storm. A less traditional example of this comes to us from my friend Lynn Levin, who ended one of her books of poetry with a list of her "Sundry Blessings." Among them is one we should recite "on being rejected by a school, an employer, or by voters": "Blessed are you, O Lord, who has not required me to change my life."[12] What at first glance might upset us, might seem dull or shabby, just might, with *kavvanah*, reveal hidden relief or even brilliance.

I once had this experience myself in New York City on *Tisha b'Av*, the day of Jewish mourning that commemorates the destruction of the Temple in ancient Jerusalem. I was walking up an avenue where they were doing street repairs, where the top layer of asphalt was scraped completely off, leaving the street scored and rough. It was not pretty. Still—again there was that undeniably religious feeling that I needed to say something in response to what I was seeing. The result was this prose poem, entitled "*Tisha b'Av*"[13] :

> They've torn the skin off my street. Underneath are the long striations of muscle tissue, but petrified; it seems possible that the city underneath us is essentially dead, that the sewage in its veins moves only for show. It might also be possible, in a long-suffering universe that reaches so casually from here to there, that the city underneath is just an old body moving on geologic time, and that I am impatient, that I am a single-celled frenetic beating against the windows of life. Meanwhile this afternoon's rain fills the striations and pours up dirty against the curb, where things are easier; meanwhile on either side of the street scaffolding rises up against the sides of these buildings bone by bone and hangs on, and then at some point each structure comes down, all the ligamenture for just an hour in shining piles along the sidewalks. The advantage

then is the sky; maybe I am walking with a book once the rain has stopped and then I realize I am blinded by the pages, and I look up through what I remember to be planks, and there it is—the fringes of the universe, soaked in some kind of blue.

This poem is about my experience of bringing *kavvanah* to something conventionally ugly and getting access to a deeper hope and beauty.

That said, in my experience, poetry and blessing are absolutely *not* about turning everything lovely. I already mentioned that there's a specific Jewish blessing people recite when they hear bad news—a setback, a rejection, a death—which translates into English as "Blessed are you, God, sovereign over the universe, the true judge." These words don't try to put a pretty gloss on things. What they do is allow us to connect to a larger reality, one beyond the hard details of the news in front of us. Just as there is a blessing for a rainbow, there is also a blessing for the storm itself.

It would be a strange person indeed who saw only good all around. After all, we're told that we are *b'tzelem elohim*, in the image of God—and God is, as we've just seen, "the true judge." That means that there is divinity in making distinctions, in eschewing rose-colored glasses in order to see the truth of things. In Afterman's words, "The Jewish way is to know the world, to deny nothing...and sing."[14] I find myself thinking of any number of psalms where the speaker is rocked with pain or despair—"Why, O God, do You forever reject us, do You fume in anger at the flock that You tend?"[15]—yet feels nonetheless compelled to sing.

The poet is sometimes in the same position. Maxine Kumin said that it was "the grit of discontent, the acute misery of early and uninformed motherhood [that] worked under [her] skin to force out the writer."[16] Natalie Goldberg, in her beloved book *Writing Down the Bones*, advised, "write *through* your pain."[17] Not away from it; not around it—*through* it. Here's another poem I wrote, this time on a particularly harrowing summer day, the poem entitled "Frustrations":

> The key freezes in the lock;
> the steps are narrow;
> the clock advances;
> the child's voice hotneedles the eardrum;

> the pack is heavy with misleading books;
> the sun is in a judgmental mood.
> The mouth is full of wind and hair,
> the belly fat but still hungry;
> the ground uneven,
> the shoes too loose,
> and everything,
> the park and street and lot,
> grown too thick with the unscalable.

If there is beauty hidden in this experience, it is not the beauty of the experience itself so much as the beauty of confronting one's emotions with clear vision and a refusal to flinch.

Whatever it is that attracts our *kavvanah*, anything from awe to horror, the effect on us is largely the same: we become awake to the world around us and the world within us. We see things with divine eyes. And so the job of the spiritual seeker and the poet—in some ways the same person by definition—is to give the world his or her devoted attention, to stay open. Allen Ginsberg once said,

> When I was young I thought I was pretty dumb, so I decided I'd better be smart and shut up and listen, and be sensitive and innocent and shy and goofy, but really pay attention to what other people said—so I listened very carefully, always worried and anxious that maybe I was getting it all wrong, or that I was too stupid to understand—and I found that, actually, the people that were smarter than me were smarter than me, and they had something to tell me, so I heard it. [18]

It's striking to see this kind of humility in a poet of Ginsberg's stature. He offers us a model of a person willing—determined, really—to learn from everyone and everything around him. In Afterman's words, "The poet has obligations—to know reality, to hold as much of the world as he can."[19]

For the poet, the blessing that results from this takes the form of a poem aware of the power in our world, a poem that brings into the light what it has discovered. Sometimes this just means telling the world what you've seen, giving it a place; Piercy has said, "I want my poems to give voice to something in the experience of a life. To find ourselves spoken for in art gives dignity to our pain, our anger, our losses."[20] In this way we actually return to the world some of what we've been given.

This sharing is a crucial step in the process. In the words of Stanley Kunitz, "In my interpretation, the poem is on its way in search of people. For its complete fulfillment it has to find an audience, it has to be invited into some other person's mind and heart."[21] Once it reaches someone else, the blessing, the ability to see the world through the eyes of the divine, naturally begins to spread.

The language of poetry itself makes that spreading easier. Poet Yehuda Amichai once said, "I personally believe that the invention, so to speak, of the metaphor is the greatest human invention, greater than the wheel or the computer." Why? "Well," he went on,

> I think first of all they're a way out of loneliness. If you use even a very worn-out metaphor or simile—for instance, you are beautiful like a rose—you are not alone. The rose becomes an equal, and it's like stretching a hand out....So I think metaphor is a reaching out.[22]

How does this work, exactly? According to literary scholar Joseph Cohen,

> The connection goes beyond that of the metaphorical function of comparing object and object or object symbol; it further establishes the crucial link between poet and reader in the *sharing* of the comparison which, when first made, enlarges the world for the poet and, subsequently, when read, does the same for the reader. [23]

Through the poem, we not only keep the world in front of our own eyes, as Falk would suggest; we keep it in front of the eyes of anyone who goes on to read the poem.

Another friend, David Guinn, is a painter and a well-loved mural artist in my hometown of Philadelphia; his work is a significant part of the urban landscape there. What this public art does is give everyone—not just those who make their way to a museum—a chance to be moved toward *kavvanah*. I know so because his mural "Summer (The Meeting),"[24] itself a piece infused with reverence, communicated its wonder to me, and provoked this poem, entitled "Mural"[25]:

> On your wall
> the moon fat and low
> a belly slung against an old undershirt
> and oh
> what a kindness
> to give us a heaven that has
> > like us
> eaten too much

In this way the blessing of *kavvanah* spreads.

It's not easy, however, to make room for all this *kavvanah*. Shapiro has noted, "If you are like most people, you are always rushing. It is as if there were a voice in your head forever urging you to hurry up. All this leaves you breathless, and breathless people are rarely spiritual people."[26] *Kavvanah* requires us to slow down. Have you ever been to a meal in an Orthodox Jewish home, experienced all the liturgy that surrounds the meal, both before and after? Similarly, have you ever walked a city block with a poet who was in the midst of a creative burst, a poet who wanted to stop at every tree or every human face? Bringing real attention to the world by necessity *un*hurries us, and at times it seems like more than we can manage.

Luckily, a little effort in this direction carries its own momentum. Approaching a meal or an acquaintance with *kavvanah* makes it easier to do it again the next time, and writing one poem can ready our mind to write the next. Piercy has suggested as much: "The more you actually see...then the more stuff you will have within you that will rise and suggest itself as imagery."[27] I think, too, of how the first day of Rosh Hashanah had instilled in me the heightened attention that would ultimately produce my poem on the second day.

And what's the alternative to *kavvanah*? *Not* noticing the world? Then what's the point of being *in* it? The Jewish tradition of the hundred blessings tells us that there *is* a point to being in the world, and that we have a responsibility to remind ourselves, and others, of that truth. The tradition of poetry tells us the same thing. From within these traditions, we can see clearly what surrounds us, what fills us, and we can know that our role is to raise our voices and sing.

Notes

1. Teutsch, Rabbi David A. (ed.). *Kol Haneshamah: Shabbat Vehagim*. Elkins Park, PA: The Reconstructionist Press, 2002, p. 208.
2. This poem first appeared in *Poetica Magazine* (2008).
3. According to Rabbi Rami Shapiro, "Depending on which period of history you read, kavvanah can mean meditation, concentration, devotion, intention, integrity of action, or attention." From his book *Minyan: Ten Principles for Living a Life of Integrity*. New York: Bell Tower, 1997, p. 106.
4. Moyers, Bill. *Fooling with Words*. New York: William Morrow & Co., 1999, p. 184.
5. Ibid., p. 198.
6. Piercy, Marge. *The Art of Blessing the Day*. New York: Knopf, 1999.
7. Teutsch, Rabbi David A. (ed.). *Kol Haneshamah: Shabbat Vehagim*. Elkins Park, PA: The Reconstructionist Press, 2002, p. 154.
8. Ibid.
9. Falk, Marcia. "Response: The Poet as Liturgist: Marcia Falk's *The Book of Blessings*," *The Reconstructionist* 62.1 (1997) p. 84.
10. Afterman, Allen. *Kabbalah and Consciousness and the Poetry of Allen Afterman*. Riverdale-on-Hudson, NY: The Sheep Meadow Press, 2005, p. 21.
11. Teutsch, Rabbi David A. (ed.). *Kol Haneshamah: Songs, Blessings and Rituals for the Home*. Wyncote, PA: The Reconstructionist Press, 1998, p. 110.
12. Levin, Lynn. *Imaginarium*. Bemidji, MN: Loonfeather Press, 2005, p. 68.
13. This poem first appeared in *Zeek Magazine* (2005).
14. Afterman, Allen. *Kabbalah and Consciousness and the Poetry of Allen Afterman*. Riverdale-on-Hudson, NY: The Sheep Meadow Press, 2005, p. 212.
15. Psalms 74:1, Jewish Publication Society translation, 1985.
16. *Writer's Almanac*. E-mail newsletter. 6 June 2008.
17. Goldberg, Natalie. *Writing Down the Bones*. Boston: Shambhala, 2005, p. 123.
18. Aronson, Jerry, dir. *The Life and Times of Allen Ginsberg*. Perf. Allen Ginsberg. 1994. DVD. New Yorker Video, 2007.
19. Afterman, Allen. *Kabbalah and Consciousness and the Poetry of Allen Afterman*. Riverdale-on-Hudson, NY: The Sheep Meadow Press, 2005, p. 208.
20. Moyers, *Fooling with Words*, p. 188.
21. Ibid., p. 12.
22. Cohen, Joseph. *Voices of Israel: Essays on and Conversations with Yehuda Amichai, A.B. Yehoshua, T. Carmi, Aharon Appelfeld and Amos Oz*. Albany, NY: State University of New York Press, 1990, p. 24.
23. Ibid.

24. Guinn, David. *Summer (The Meeting)*. Mario Lanza park, 2nd and Queen Streets, Philadelphia, PA.
25. This poem first appeared in *Phoebe* 33:2 (2004) 89.
26. Shapiro, Rabbi Rami M. *Minyan: Ten Principles for Living a Life of Integrity*. New York: Bell Tower, 1997, p. 108.
27. Moyers, *Fooling with Words*, pp. 179-180.

SIMONE WEIL'S ETHIC OF THE OTHER
Explicating Fictions through Fiction, or
Looking through the Wrong End of the Telescope

Ruthann Knechel Johansen

> When the "power of the social element" usurps God's place in the soul, the collective soul is ascendant. "The collective is the object of all idolatry, this it is which chains us to the earth."[1]
>
> Idolatry is due to the fact that, while athirst for absolute good, one is not in possession of supernatural attention; and one has not the patience to let it grow.[2]

I.

Asbury Fox and Ruby Turpin, two characters in Flannery O'Connor's twentieth century fiction—the first facing a slide toward death and the other self-righteously ascending toward heaven on her virtues—illustrate the characteristics and dangers of collectivities that French philosopher Simone Weil regarded, along with force, to undergird all forms of oppression, including colonialism. Both Weil and O'Connor lived and worked—as do we—in the midst of powerful collectives; and each attempted to discern the operations from within them. Weil sought to understand and interpret through philosophical reflection the economic, political, cultural, and religious idolatries that coalesce in collectivities. O'Connor deferred to art and irony to disclose the legacies inherited from such collectivities as slavery and imperialism.

As a literary scholar indebted to Simone Weil's thought and to the work of Weil scholars, I read the philosopher and the American fiction writer in each other's light for the mutual illumination they provide on each other's work and together offer for contemporary reflection, as citizens and governments confront residues of nineteenth and twentieth century colonialism and new threats of imperialism. Weil's "The Colonial Question and the Destiny of the French People" and "Human Personality" (also translated "The Sacredness of the Person"), written within a year of each other and two O'Connor short stories—"The Enduring Chill" and "Revelation"—form the foundation for this analysis.

Two provocative statements made by Weil, one in "The Colonial Question" and the other in "Human Personality," inspire this examination of the relationship between collectivities and oppression. Written as response to the devastating threat of Hitler, not only in France but also across Europe, Weil argues in "The Colonial Question" that there can be no hope for the future of the human species without reconsidering colonial practices and the temptations on which those practices rest.[3] In "Human Personality," where Weil distills her observations about all forms of injustice into conclusions about the human person and investigates the relationship between individuals who compose a collectivity and the power of the collectivity as a whole, she asserts

> it is useless to explain to a collectivity that there is something in each of the units composing it which it ought not to violate. To begin with, a collectivity is not someone, except by a fiction; it has only an abstract existence and can only be spoken to fictitiously. And, moreover, if it were someone it would be someone who was not disposed to respect anything except himself.[4]

In her aesthetic described in "Morality and Literature," Weil explains that her idea that fiction generates immorality is not confined to literature. She says that "the substance of our life is almost exclusively composed of fiction. We fictionalize our future; and, unless we are heroically devoted to truth, we fictionalize our past, refashioning it to our taste. We do not study other people; we *invent* [emphasis added] what they are thinking, saying, and doing."[5] The perils of collectivities as fictions lead to my thesis: Explicating collectivities as fictions through fiction (1) illumines their roles in various forms of oppression and (2) points toward the need for detachment from social idolatries so that fuller alignment with the supernatural becomes possible.

My decision to draw upon two Flannery O'Connor stories to develop the thesis of this essay is prompted by statements made by Weil in "The Colonial Question and the Destiny of the French People" that "the loss of the past is equivalent to the loss of the supernatural" and by her assertion that America's lack of sympathy for the colonial system because it has "no colonies, and as a consequence no colonial prejudices. . ." might help the French find a meaning for the word *protection* of the weak or the subjected that is not a falsehood. She perceived this potential aid coming from America's tendency naively "to apply her democratic criteria to everything that does not concern her directly."[6] By taking the side of the oppressed, Weil thought, America challenges Europeans ensnared in colonialism and, if Europeans realize it, can even help Europeans resist negative American influence in the future.

Weil's interpretation of the United States' relationship to colonialism falls short in two ways that Flannery O'Connor can paradoxically at least enlarge if not correct: First, Weil understates the ways America has been implicated in forms of colonization through the displacement of the native Americans; its policy of Manifest Destiny; its quasi-imperial relationship with Cuba, the Philippines, and other Latin American countries following the Spanish-American War; and its own complicity in European colonialism during U.S. importation of slaves from West Africa. Second, she overlooks how these factors contributed to the United States fictionalizing its own past, to displacing or severing connection to the supernatural, and to the enduring consequences of that sacrifice. The conditions that contribute to the loss of connection to the past and to the supernatural, and that hence undergird all oppressions, are laid out in "Human Personality" and provide the foundation on which the analysis of O'Connor's "The Enduring Chill" and "Revelation" is constructed.

II.
In "Human Personality," Weil distinguishes between the person or personality and the impersonal, which is what is sacred in every human being. A grave error in language and thought, known as Personalism, seduces human beings into identifying with their personalities, becoming attached to language that imprisons the mind in error, and submerging one's

being in a collectivity. Although personalities can produce dazzling achievements in science, art, and philosophy, and can even attempt to extend the limits of those things that create suffering, such achievements are "separated by an abyss" from "the level where the highest [essentially anonymous] things are achieved."[7] Personalities depend upon social prestige for inflation, which suggests why ". . . upheavals like war and civil war are so intoxicating; they empty human lives of their reality and seem to turn people into puppets. That is also why slavery is so pleasant to masters," argues Weil. The reliance on social affirmation or prestige makes human beings vulnerable to collectives, and experiencing the impersonal in collectives is impossible. For Weil, "the collectivity is not only alien to the sacred, but it deludes us with a false imitation of it. Idolatry is the name of the error which attributes a sacred character to the collectivity; and it is the commonest of crimes, at all times, at all places."[8]

Why Weil considered collectivities fictions can be inferred from careful readings not only of her essays on colonialism but also of her critiques of Marxism or of social life, her "Theoretical Picture of a Free Society," and of additional essays on "The Power of Words," "Morality and the Literature," and her "Draft for a Statement of Human Obligations."[9] She warned against collectivities because first they are abstract and promote abstractions. Second, they depend for their life on blind allegiance of those who, by submerging their personalities in them, lose touch with the impersonal. Third, collectivities rely on "mind[s] [that] can possess only opinions" not thoughts. Fourth, they discourage reflection and weaken the linkage between thought and actions. Fifth, as Weil said of force, both those who dominate in a collectivity and those who are in servitude to it are intellectually, emotionally, and ethically enslaved. Sixth, ultimately, collectivities substitute false reality for true reality, and false reality can only be broken through when individuals in a collectivity are returned to their separate selves. In Weil's words, "although the personal and the impersonal are opposed, there is a way from the one to the other. But there is no way from the collective to the impersonal."[10] To reach the impersonal, "a collectivity must dissolve into separate persons. . . . [I]mpersonality is only reached by the practice of a form of attention which is rare in itself and impossible except in solitude, and not only physical but mental solitude."[11] Justice, truth, and beauty are the images in our world of the impersonal. Weil believed that because the love of truth must be accompanied by humility, not pride, the only way into truth was through one's own annihilation or decreation.[12] Indeed, she concludes in "Human Personality" that "there is no guarantee for democracy, or for the protection of the person against the collectivity, without a disposition of public life relating it to the higher good which is impersonal and unrelated to any political form."[13]

III.

Had Simone Weil associated the United States with colonialism through the displacement of Native Americans and its own importation of slaves from colonized regions of West Africa, she would have further buttressed her argument that unreflective efforts to alleviate one form of oppression usually beget other oppressive behaviors. Paradoxically, Flannery O'Connor, herself rooted in the historically slave-dependent U.S. South and frequently charged by late twentieth and twenty-first-century critics of supporting racist attitudes in her fiction, illustrates as she complicates the behaviors Weil associated with collectivities. This becomes clear by explicating the stories through the characteristics Weil attributed to collectivities. In "The Enduring Chill" and "Revelation," O'Connor illustrates how racism, classism, and materialism represent interwoven collectivities—bearing the characteristics against which Weil warned—that sever human beings from the past and the supernatural.

In the opening paragraph of "The Enduring Chill," O'Connor hints at Asbury Fox's attraction to abstractions when the young intellectual dismounts from the train in his home town of Timberboro and "felt that he was about to witness a majestic transformation, that the flat of roofs might at any moment turn into the mounting turrets of some exotic temple for a god he didn't know. The illusion lasted only a moment before his attention was drawn back to his mother."[14] Asbury has been living in New York trying to invent himself as a writer and preoccupied with absorbing Art and Culture. Although neither his mother nor his sister Mary George can understand Asbury's aesthetic temperament, they both feed his abstract construction of himself as an artist: His mother confesses inwardly that "she simply didn't understand how it felt to be sensitive or how peculiar you were when you were an artist," whereas "Mary George had said that if Asbury had had any talent, he would by now have published something. What had he ever published, she wanted to know, and for that matter, what had he ever written?"[15] While in New York other abstractions like Buddhism's concept of illusion, which he was not prepared to accept, also attracted him, and then he settled his fascination on a Jesuit priest "who appealed to him as a man of the world, someone who would have understood the unique tragedy of his death...."[16]

Suffering severe chills and exhaustion when he returns to Timberboro, Asbury is convinced that he is dying. Now Death, knocking on his body, becomes his consuming abstraction. Before leaving New York, he had written a letter, imitating another artist, which filled two notebooks—"it was such a letter as Kafka had addressed to his father"—that his mother was not meant to read until after his death, although he expected her literal mind would not understand it at once.[17]

> If reading it would be painful to her, writing it had sometimes been unbearable to him—for in order to face her, he had had to face himself. "I came here to escape the slave's atmosphere of home . . . to find freedom, to liberate my imagination, to take it like a hawk from its cage and set it 'whirling off into the widening gyre' (Yeats) and what did I find? It was incapable of flight. . . . I have no imagination. I have no talent. I can't create. I have nothing but the desire for these things. Why didn't you kill that too? Woman, why did you pinion me?"[18]

Although he privately assures himself that he was becoming accustomed to the thought of death, "he had not become accustomed to the thought of death *here* [at home in what his sister calls the artist's gas chamber]."[19] That Death is an abstraction for Asbury becomes clear when he vociferously refuses, but then resentfully relents, his mother's suggestion that she will call the local Dr. Block who will take a *personal* interest in him.

Asbury's refusal of personal attention suggests the extent to which he has merged his personality with idealizations or collectivities. As a liberal angered by the narrow, racist worldview of his mother, he attempts to abandon his Methodist past in his idealization of a religious collective (the Jesuits) and to transgress racial and class boundaries by inviting his mother's black farmhands into a new social order. On a previous visit home, when he had been writing a play about Negroes and wanted to work in the dairy with the farmhands "to find out what their interests were,"[20] he invited Randall and Morgan, whom he cannot tell apart, to smoke with him. When the creamery returns the milk the following day "because it had absorbed the odor of tobacco, it is the Negroes Mrs. Fox blames, not her son. Pressing further against the established prohibitions, Asbury later pours fresh, warm milk into the jelly glass out of which the Negroes drink, downs it quickly, pours another, and offers them fresh, warm milk to drink with him in a secular Eucharist. They refuse, saying, "That *the* thing she don't 'low."[21] By appropriating symbols of religious submission and salvific rites with Asbury's liberal, largely secular vision of a more enlightened order in which "the difference between black and white is absorbed into nothing,"[22] O'Connor illustrates how the long-lost past of these descendants of the slave system—farmhands and owner alike—impinges on the present and can obliterate the supernatural.

Those who are submerged in collectivities, Weil suggests, rely on opinions, not on ideas, and the links between their thought and actions are weak. Asbury holds a highly opinionated view of his mother's attitudes and his sister, whom he believed "posed as an intellectual but that her I.Q. couldn't be over seventy-five, that all she was really interested in was getting a man but that no sensible man would finish a first look at her."[23] His opinions about his mother's racial practices and prejudices permit him to repudiate his own past in preference for his liberal enlightenment and to submit Randall and Morgan to moral abuse by using them to fulfill his own arrogant liberalism. When Asbury tries to persuade Randall to drink the forbidden milk, he counsels, "We've got to think free if we want to live free." This invitation is extended to the oppressed by an oppressor who can't live free himself from his idealized abstractions, including his subsequent obsession with death, and who fails to think that his action of drinking unpasteurized milk may contribute to his present physical condition. O'Connor exposes Asbury's reliance on opinion and the failure to link thought and action through ironic subversion when Randall and Morgan, invited by Asbury to his bedroom to say final good-byes, mock and resist his moral abuse through flattery adopted as a collective response to bondage:

> "You sho do look well," Randall said. "You looks very well."
> "You looks well," the other one said. "Yessuh, you looks fine."

"I ain't ever seen you looking so well before," Randall said, . . .
"I speck you ain't even sick."[24]

Throughout "The Enduring Chill," Flannery O'Connor depicts the ways those who dominate and those in servitude—mother over son, son over mother, whites over blacks, blacks subverting whites, doctors and priests over the suffering—are usually entrapped in collectivities that have "an abstract existence and can only be spoken to fictitiously."[25] In this story, intersecting collectivities of racism, liberalism, and secularism, all bound to the legacy of slavery, impinge on the family and distort each individual's view of reality. Vulnerability to substituting false realities for true reality begins with Mrs. Fox's emphasis on Asbury's need for *personal* attention. As Weil argues, focusing on the personal or personality obstructs the view of the whole person, the sacred impersonal. Trapped in personalism, Asbury elevates a curable disease to grand end-of-life suffering. Indeed, he confuses self-induced illness, the symptoms of which he rehearses *ad nauseam*, with affliction. His preoccupation with dying and being uprooted from life remains, until Dr. Block's revelation, a false decreation because he remains at the center of his own attention and his narrow world. Dr. Block's verdict that Asbury is suffering from undulant fever arrives like an epiphany; his false view of his situation is stripped away; the collectivities in which he has submerged himself are at least exposed, if not dissolved, and Asbury saw that

> The old life in him was exhausted. He awaited the coming of the new. . . . His breath came short. The fierce bird which through the years of his childhood and the days of his illness had been poised over his head [as a water stain on the ceiling], waiting mysteriously, appeared all at once to be in motion. Asbury blanched and the last film of illusion was torn as if by a whirlwind from his eyes. He saw that for the rest of his days, frail, racked, but enduring, he would live in the face of a purifying terror. A feeble cry, a last impossible protest escaped him. But the Holy Ghost, emblazoned in ice instead of fire, continued, implacable, to descend.[26]

Flannery O'Connor's "Revelation" embodies further the power collectivities hold over human beings and the virtually cataclysmic clash she thought necessary to wrest individuals from partial or false reality. In this story, the major collectivities threaded throughout include classism, racism, and religious fanaticism through which Ruby Turpin secures herself in her world. With husband Claud in tow, Mrs. Turpin arrives in the waiting room of the doctor's office as a big woman whose personal emphasis on her good disposition abstractly sets her apart—a little larger than life—from others in the room. Preoccupied with abstractions, she assesses and classifies people quickly through their shoes, posture, cleanliness, and language and the stereotypes she associates with each of those criteria. For example, O'Connor writes,

> Without appearing to, Mrs. Turpin always noticed people's feet [that which binds people to the earth]. The well-dressed lady had on red and grey suede shoes to match her dress. Mrs. Turpin had on her good black patent leather pumps. The ugly girl had on Girl Scout shoes and heavy socks. The old woman had on tennis shoes and the white-trashy mother had on what appeared to be bedroom slippers, black straw with gold braid threaded through them—exactly what you would have expected her to have on.[27]

At night when she can't sleep, Mrs. Turpin occupies herself naming the classes of people.

> On the bottom of the heap were most colored people. . . ; then next to them—not above, just away from—were the white-trash; then above them were the home-owners, to which she and Claud belonged. Above she and Claud were people with a lot of money and much bigger houses and much more land. But here the complexity of it would begin to bear in on her, for some of the people with a lot of money were common and ought to be below she and Claud and some of the people who had good blood had lost their money and had to rent and then there were colored people who owned their homes and land as well.[28]

Mrs. Turpin secures her personal identity by locating herself in her system of social classifications and expects acknowledgment, if not allegiance, from others of her superior status. When the woman she regards as white trash enters the conversation with her opinion that "hogs [are] nasty stinking things, a-gruntin and a-rootin all over the place," Mrs. Turpin asserts her dominant position by retorting, "Our hogs are not dirty and they don't stink. They're cleaner than some children I've seen. Their feet never touch the ground. We have a pig parlor—that's where you raise them on concrete . . . and Claud scoots them down with the hose every afternoon and washes off the floor."[29] Her attitude toward their Negroes exposes further her allegiance to racial categories and her conviction of her own racial superiority, as she tells the stylish woman, "I sure am tired of buttering up niggers, but you got to love em if you want em to work for you. When they come in the morning, I run out and I say, 'Hi yawl this morning?' And when Claud drives them off to the field I just wave to beat the band and they just wave back."[30]

Mrs. Turpin's reliance on opinions rather than carefully considered ideas is most visible in the way she personalizes her religious beliefs, and her self-righteous opinions precipitate the violent eruption from Mary Grace, the Wellesley student reading the book entitled *Human Development*. Internal rationalizing and hypothesizing about who others in the waiting room are and what they think or feel undergird the free sharing of stereotypes; even one stereotypic opinion subverts another as the following exchange among Turpin, Mary Grace's mother, and the white trash woman suggests,

> "They ought to send all them niggers back to Africa," the white-trash woman said. "That's wher they come from in the first place."
> "Oh, I couldn't do without my good colored friends," the pleasant lady said.
> "There's a heap of things worse than a nigger," Mrs. Turpin agreed. "It's all kinds of them just like it's all kinds of us. . . ."
> "It wouldn't be practical to send them back to Africa," [Mrs. Turpin] said.
> "Wouldn't be what they wanted—if I had anythang to do with it," the woman said.
> "It wouldn't be a way in the world you could get all the niggers back over there," Mrs. Turpin said. "They'd be hiding out and lying down and turning sick on you and wailing and hollering and

raring and pitching. It wouldn't be a way in the world to get them over there."[31]

The moral abuse that Mrs. Turpin exerts through her opinions of herself and her categorizing of others and that provokes the physical abuse that Mary Grace hurls against Mrs. Turpin are tied together by Mrs. Turpin's religious assumptions that are highly personal and preferential.

Reflecting to herself, she muses

> If Jesus had said, "you can be high society and have all the money you want and be thin and svelte-like, but you can't be a good woman with it," she would have had to say, "Well don't make me that then. Make me a good woman and it don't matter what else, how fat or how ugly or how poor!" Her heart rose. He had not made her a nigger or white-trash or ugly! He had made her herself and given her a little of everything. Jesus, thank you! she said. Thank you, thank you, thank you! Whenever she counted her blessings she felt as buoyant as if she weighed one hundred and twenty-five pounds instead of one hundred and eighty.[32]

The weak link between her thought and actions that have been suggested throughout the story are challenged when Mary Grace's *Human Development* book hits Mrs. Turpin squarely above her left eye. When her head clears and her ability to move returns, Mrs. Turpin looks straight at Mary Grace and asked, "What you got to say to me?" To which the girl replies, "Go back to hell where you came from, you old wart hog."[33] This physical force visited upon Mrs. Turpin requires her throughout the remainder of the story to rethink, or perhaps think for the first time, about her position and beyond her personality. Lying in bed when she arrives home she asks, "How am I a wart hog from hell and myself too?" And later she considers the question again as she surveys the hogs in the hog parlor.

As in "The Enduring Chill" so here in "Revelation," O'Connor depicts the mutual bondage of both those who dominate and those who are dominated. Taking water to the Negroes coming back in the truck, she greets them with her usual friendliness, but when they see the dark protuberance over her eye, inquire about it, and she regales them with the events, the Negroes flatter her with their sympathy and compliments on her sweetness and prettiness. Previously dependent on such obeisance, now Mrs. Turpin is irritated, for "[she] knew just exactly how much Negro flattery was worth and it added to her rage."[34] As a result of the attack, the flattery which for the blacks may be a form of resistance to bondage serves further to break through the collectivity of racism in which both the Negroes and Mrs. Turpin have been entrapped.

With the assault of Mary Grace's text book, Mrs. Turpin's own arrested human development is challenged. As the girl's fingers clamped into the soft flesh of Mrs. Turpin's neck "all at once her vision narrowed and she saw everything as if it were happening in a small room far away, or as if she were looking at it through the wrong end of a telescope."[35] The confrontation of her personality, submerged in the collectivities of race, class, and religious self-righteousness, outrages her as she speaks to a more vast, less personal God while hosing down the pigs at the end of the day. "What do you send me a message like that for?" And she continued,

> "Why me?" she rumbled. "It's no trash around here, black or white, that I haven't given to. And break my back to the bone every day working. And do for the church. . . . How am I a hog?" she demanded. "There's plenty of trash there. It didn't have to be me. If you like trash better, go get yourself some trash then," she railed. "You could have made me trash. Or a nigger. If trash is what you wanted why didn't you make me trash?. . . Or you could have made me a nigger. It's too late for me to be a nigger," she said with deep sarcasm, "but I could act like one. Lay down in the middle of the road and stop traffic. Roll on the ground. . . . Go on, . . . call me a hog! Call me a hog again. From hell. Call me a wart hog from hell. Put that bottom rail on top. There'll still be a top and bottom."[36]

In a final surge of fury she roared, "Who do you think you are?" The question echoed across the pasture "and returned to her clearly like an answer from beyond the sound."[37]

In her final vision over the pig pen Mrs. Turpin sees

> . . . a vast swinging bridge extending upward from the earth through a field of living fire. Upon it a vast horde of souls were

rumbling toward heaven. There were whole companies of white-trash, clean for the first time in their lives, and bands of black niggers in white robes, and battalions of freaks and lunatics shouting and clapping and leaping like frogs. And bringing up the end of the procession was a tribe of people whom she recognized at once as those who, like herself and Claud, had always had a little of everything and the God-given wit to use it right . . . she could see by their shocked and altered faces that even their virtues were being burned away.[38]

In her humiliation that approximates affliction for her, Mrs. Turpin's identification with the collectivities of race, class, and religious piety has been shattered. Her false view of reality has been radically altered, turned upside down, so that she may enter the "realm of the real," which Simone Weil described to Joe Bousquet, a poet and crippled veteran of the First World War in these words:

The egg is this world we see. The bird in it is Love, the Love which is God himself and which lives in the depths of every man, though at first as an invisible seed. When the shell is broken and the being is released, it still has this same world before it. But it is no longer inside. Space is opened and torn apart. The spirit, leaving the miserable body in some corner, is transported to a point outside space, which is not a point of view, which has no perspective, but from which the world is seen as it is. . . .[39]

IV.
While Simone Weil discussed with analytic acuity the physical and moral abuses that accompany injustices and inequality inflicted upon factory workers or colonized peoples through force and submission, Flannery O'Connor satirized the excesses of human personalities trapped in collectivities in rural Georgia, a regionless region that is everywhere and separated from the supernatural. Although working in different genres, Weil and O'Connor looked down the wrong end of the telescope to help us view near things in the reality of distance, of the transcendent. Writing in *Mystery and Manners*, O'Connor says,

> All novelists are fundamentally seekers and describers of the real, but the realism of each novelist will depend on his view of the ultimate reaches of reality. . . if the writer believes that our life is and will remain essentially mysterious, if he looks upon us as beings existing in a created order to whose laws we freely respond, then what he sees on the surface will be of interest to him only as he can go through it into an experience of mystery itself.[40]

O'Connor's vision of human beings is prophetic in ways similar to Weil's vision, for both had the capacity to see through surfaces to something transcendent or eternal. Although O'Connor's characters are often comic and grotesque, she asserts that "they carry an invisible burden; their fanaticism is a reproach not merely an eccentricity," for "in the novelist's case prophecy is a matter of seeing near things with their extensions of meaning and thus of seeing far things close up."[41] Using the image of the telescope, J. P. Little remarks, in her introduction to *Simone Weil on Colonialism*, on Weil's ability to make a direct comparison between France's conquest of peripheral regions of France throughout French history to Hitler's designs on Europe. Like novelist O'Connor,

> Weil demonstrates . . . her remarkable capacity to go beyond a narrow nationalism and the restricted point of view either of the self-centered individual or of the collective. Indeed, one of her most notable contributions to the whole colonization debate, as it was manifest in her times, is her ability to look down the other end of the telescope, to become, literally, "the Other."[42]

To look down the wrong end of the telescope, an image used by O'Connor and of Weil, suggests that one sees those things that are nearest, most consuming, threatening, or powerful—including one's personality and vested interests—as distant or small. Such a shift in perspective separates one from one's personality and others from the inventions or fictions in which they have clothed themselves or been clothed by others. Theoretically, the shift permits a glimpse of the impersonal, from the distance of the supernatural, in oneself and in others. To recognize the presence of the impersonal in another human being is the first step toward what I regard as Weil's ethic of the Other; the second is to become the other through one's embrace of her own impersonality. The significance of this recognition and embrace is profound for social orders and for reality, as Weil suggests in the *Notebooks*: "Any man who is in contact with the supernatural is essentially king, for he represents the presence in society, in the form of something infinitely small, of an order transcending the social order.... He is a centre of gravity *in* that position."[43]

Approaching the impersonal is fraught with utmost challenge, for attention must be "turned lovingly toward God (or, in a lesser degree toward anything that is truly beautiful)" and away from patriotism, slavery, modern totalitarianisms, including religious totalitarianism and secularism, and "service of the false God (or of the Social Beast in whatever form it may be)," asserts Weil in her *Notebooks*.[44] In addition to giving one's attention to beauty, one can approach the impersonal through justice and truth as images in our world of the impersonal. As an artist, not a philosopher, Flannery O'Connor associated art with truth and followed St. Thomas who was concerned about the good of that which is made and called art "reason in making." Like Weil, O'Connor was cautious about the word *art*, saying "Art is a word that immediately scares people off, as being a little too grand. But all I mean by art is writing something that is valuable in itself and that works in itself. The basis of art is truth, both in matter and mode. The person who aims after art in his work aims after truth, in an imaginative sense, no more and no less."[45] O'Connor surrendered her attention to art that would disclose truth. She says

> the artist uses his reason to discover an answering reason in everything he sees. For him, to be reasonable is to find, in the object, in the situation, in the sequence, the spirit which makes it itself. This is not an easy or simple thing to do. It is to intrude upon the timeless, and that is only done by the violence of a single-minded respect for the truth.[46]

Although never writing of personalism or the impersonal in the way Simone Weil does in "Human Personality," Flannery O'Connor does recognize how identification with one's personality obscures the impersonal and the reality of the supernatural. She asserts that "it is usually some form of self-inflation that destroys the free use of a gift.

This may be the pride of the reformer or the theorist, or it may only be that simple-minded self-appreciation which uses its own sincerity as a standard for truth."[47] O'Connor's underlinings in her copy of *Modern Man in Search of a Soul* by Carl Jung, a psychoanalytic theorist whom she thought more dangerous than Freud, suggest her suspicion of the personal and her understanding of the relationship between art and the supernatural. She had underlined the following sentences:

> The personal aspect is a limitation—and even a sin—in the realm of art. When a form of "art" is primarily personal it deserves to be treated as if it were a neurosis. [For Jung and O'Connor], . . . art is a kind of innate drive that seizes a human being and makes him its instrument. The artist is not a person endowed with free will who seeks his own ends, but one who allows art to realize its purposes through him. As a human being he may have moods and a will and personal aims, but as an artist he is "man" in a higher sense. . . .[48]

In "Morality and Literature," in which O'Connor makes immorality an aesthetic criterion because by confusing good and evil it gives us unreality, Weil allows that there are writers of genius whose works "are outside the realm of fiction and they release us from it. They give us, in the guise of fiction, something equivalent to the actual density of the real, that density which life offers us every day but which we are unable to grasp because we are amusing ourselves with lies."[49] I will not argue that O'Connor fits Weil's category of genius, but her fiction does point, through shallow and obsessional characters alike, both those who hunger and thirst for the supernatural and those who resist or distort it, toward the density life offers.

By explicating the fictions of collectivities, Weil and O'Connor reveal that "the collectivity is not only alien to the sacred, but it deludes us with a false imitation of it."[50] While Weil explains that in order for the impersonal, the sacred in each human being, to be reached the collectivity must be dissolved, O'Connor shows the radical, often violent, *metanoia* that occurs within the human soul as it separates from the collectivity, and the false reality the collectivity sustains, to align itself with the transcendent. Paradoxically, only in separation—or, as Weil suggests, most frequently through affliction or uprooting of oneself—do the people and things of this world become *metaxu*, bridges, links, or intermediaries to the supernatural, the world of God. Weil's and O'Connor's explication of collectivity makes visible the historical legacies of and contemporary commitment to social idolatries that sustain all forms of oppression and unleash endless contests of force in the world. To move toward the impersonal and to be aligned with the supernatural requires detachment from our personalities and idolatrous collectivities. When such detachment, or uprooting, is possible, Weil suggests, one can see that

> the true earthly blessings are *metaxu*. We can respect those of others in so far as we regard those we ourselves possess as *metaxu*. This implies that we are already making our way toward the point where it is possible to do without them. For example, if we are to respect foreign countries, we must make of our own country not an idol, but a steppingstone toward God.[51]

Explicating collectivities as fictions theoretically makes it possible for earthly blessings to be experienced as *metaxu*—as bridges of the Greeks—and not turned into idols used to defend collective interests. On the *metaxu* one must not erect houses or skyscrapers, suggests Weil, or, I would add, construct social ladders reaching into the heavens, or build military arsenals that imperil the earth and the Other with whom each individual, in truth and dignity, is bound to All.

Works cited

Jung, C. G., 1933, *Modern Man in Search of a Soul*, New York: Harcourt Brace & World.

Little, J. P., 2003, *Simone Weil on Colonialism: An Ethic of the Other*, Oxford: Rowman & Littlefield.

Miles, Sian, 1986, Ed. and Trans. *Simone Weil: An Anthology*. New York: Grove Press.

O'Connor, Flannery, 1988, *Flannery O'Connor: Collected Works*. New York: Library of America.

O'Connor, Flannery, 1957, *Mystery and Manners,* Sally Fitzgerald, ed. New York: Farrar, Strauss and Giroux.

Panichas, George A., ed., 1977, *The Simone Weil Reader*, Wakefield, RI: Moyer Bell.

Weil, Simone, 1997, *Oeuvres complètes. Tome VI, volume 3, K9 ms 65, 34*. Andre A. Devaux, and Florence de Lussy, ed. Paris: Gallimard.

Weil, Simone, 1958, *Oppression and Liberty*. Trans. Arthur Wills, and John Petrie. Amherst: University of Massachusetts Press.

Weil, Simone, 1962, *Selected Essays 1934–1943*. Ed. and Trans. Richard Rees. London: Oxford University Press.

Notes

1. George A. Panichas, ed., 1977, *The Simone Weil Reader*, Wakefield, RI: Moyer Bell, 391.
2. Simone Weil, *Oeuvres complètes,* Tome VI, volume 3, K9 ms 65, in Andre A. Devaux and Florence de Lussy, ed., Paris: Gallimard, 1997, 204.
3. The practices that Weil mentions include: patriotism that prefers its own country to justice; reliance upon experts, in this case the colonials, whose judgment is not impartial; and Christian belief that weds colonization with missions.
4. Simone Weil, 1962, *Selected Essays 1934–1943*, London: Oxford University Press, 16.
5. Simone Weil, "Morality and Literature," *Simone Weil Reader,* 292.
6. Simone Weil, 2003, "The Colonial Question and the Destiny of the French People," J.P. Little, ed. and trans., *Simone Weil on Colonialism: An Ethic of the Other*, Oxford: Rowman & Littlefield, 118.
7. Weil, "Human Personality," 13.
8. Weil, "Human Personality," 14.
9. See for example Weil's "Theoretical Picture of a Free Society" in *Oppression and Liberty*, trans. Arthur Wills and John Petrie, Amherst: University of Massachusetts Press, 1958, 1973; "The Power of Words," "The Great Beast," "Draft for a Statement of Human Obligations" in Richard Rees, ed. and trans., *Selected Essays 1934–1943*, London: Oxford University Press, 1962; "Morality in Literature" in George A. Panichas, ed., *The Simone Weil Reader*, Wakefield, RI: Moyer Bell, 1977.
10. Weil, "Human Personality," 14.
11. Weil, "Human Personality," 14.
12. See Weil's essay "Decreation" in *The Simone Weil Reader*, 350–6. Decreation is a spiritual act of making "something created pass into the uncreated. . . . It is necessary to uproot oneself. . . . We must take the feeling of being at home into exile. We must be rooted in the absence of a place."
13. Weil, "Human Personality," 34.
14. Flannery O'Connor, 1988, "The Enduring Chill," *Flannery O'Connor: Collected Works*, New York: Library of America, 547.
15. O'Connor, "The Enduring Chill," 552–3.
16. O'Connor, "The Enduring Chill," 550.
17. O'Connor, "The Enduring Chill," 554.
18. O'Connor, "The Enduring Chill," 554.
19. O'Connor, "The Enduring Chill," 548.
20. O'Connor, "The Enduring Chill," 551.
21. O'Connor, "The Enduring Chill," 559.
22. O'Connor, "The Enduring Chill," 558.
23. O'Connor, "The Enduring Chill," 553.

24. O'Connor, "The Enduring Chill," 569.
25. Weil, "Human Personality," 16.
26. O'Connor, "The Enduring Chill," 572.
27. O'Connor, "Revelation," 635.
28. O'Connor, "Revelation," 636.
29. O'Connor, "Revelation," 638.
30. O'Connor, "Revelation," 639.
31. O'Connor, "Revelation," 640–41.
32. O'Connor, "Revelation," 642.
33. O'Connor, "Revelation," 646.
34. O'Connor, "Revelation," 650.
35. O'Connor, "Revelation," 644.
36. O'Connor, "Revelation, 652–53.
37. O'Connor, "Revelation," 653.
38. O'Connor, "Revelation," 654.
39. Sian Miles, ed. and trans., "Introduction, *Simone Weil: An Anthology*, New York: Grove Press, 1986, 43–44.
40. Flannery O'Connor, "The Grotesque in Southern Fiction," *Mystery and Manners*, ed. Sally Fitzgerald, New York: Farrar, Straus and Giroux, 1957, 40-41.
41. O'Connor, "The Grotesque in Southern Fiction," 44.
42. J. P. Little, ed., *Simone Weil on Colonialism: An Ethic of the Other*, 19.
43. Weil, *Oeuvres complètes* VI, K9 ms 34, 180.
44. Weil, *Oeuvres complètes* VI-3, K9 ms 65, 204.
45. O'Connor, "The Nature and Aim of Fiction," *Mystery and Manners*, 65.
46. O'Connor, "The Nature and Aim of Fiction," 82–83.
47. O'Connor, "The Nature and Aim of Fiction," 82.
48. C. G. Jung, 1933, *Modern Man in Search of a Soul*, New York: Harcourt Brace & World, 194–95.
49. Weil, "Morality and Literature," 292.
50. Weil, "Human Personality," 14.
51. Weil, "Metaxu," in Panichas, 365.

DIVINE EXPLORATION AND INVITATION

L. B. C. Keefe-Perry

In a recent essay,[1] Eric McLuhan reiterates the argument that his late father, Marshall McLuhan, oft-termed a media theorist, worked without the use of theories. He supports this claim by suggesting that while his father did use theories, he did not use them in a consistent way. Rather than attempting to develop a culminating thesis, the elder McLuhan was more interested in the work of aphorism and art than explication and exegesis: he was most content when probing and observing, asking questions and exploring. This elusive and playful spirit of inquiry and expression has been the inspiration for much of my own work and is at the heart of the essay you now read. I write to share with you some ideas I have discovered in my own journey and will not consider it a failure should this piece raise more questions than it answers. Those looking for a more exhaustive and traditional treatment of theopoetics are encouraged to see my recent piece in *Christianity & Literature*[2] or the website I maintain, http://theopoetics.net.

> It is a matter of how you begin: if you begin with theory, then one way or another your research winds up geared to making the case for or against the truth of the theory. Begin with theory, you begin with the answer; begin with observation, you begin with questions. A theory always turns into a scientist's point of view and a way of seeing the job at hand. Begin with observation and your task is to look at things and to look at what happens. To see.
>
> —Eric McLuhan[3]

> The explorer is totally inconsistent. He never knows at what moment he will make some startling discovery. And consistency is a meaningless term to apply to an explorer. If he wanted to be consistent he would stay home.
>
> —Marshall McLuhan[4]

Observation

I recently found myself alone in a motel, staring at a jacuzzi in a hot room that smelled of stale cigarettes. It was nearly two in the morning, and the bathroom had no walls. I presume this design element was included so that one's bathing experience might also include ease of access to the bedroom, which, I might add, contained a genuine Magic Fingers® bed. The event of this encounter served as yet another opportunity to test my belief that it serves every person of faith to try to find God however they might in the place and time of their situation. As it grew nearer to 3 am and my place remained a less than desirable hotel, I struggled to make meaning of it all.

I have been a school teacher by training and occupation, and it was a job interview that had landed me in my aforementioned surroundings. I had missed a connection to Rochester, New York in the labryntine glory of the John Fitzgerald Kennedy International Airport, and was told that the next flight would not be until the following morning. Thirteen phone calls later, I had discovered that (1) late-night airport hotel finding is not for the easily discouraged, (2) that the kindness of strangers sometimes is real, and (3) that "the great cash only special" is neither great nor special in any standard use of those words.

Having been delayed for hours aboard my New York bound flight, and having had to attempt communications to my potential employers via cell phone at midnight, I was more than ready to accept the advice of a local who "knew a place." One handwritten address, a pleasant urban cab ride, and a snarky glance from our cabbie later, another stranded traveler and I ended up at our destination. After some confusion regarding the fact that we would not be sharing a room, the night shift employee pointed me toward my accommodations and I was allowed to stand in slack-jawed awe of the my jacuzzi-appointed furnishings. I told myself I had some work to do to figure out what the larger point of this fiasco was. Six hours later, on board a flight I was never "supposed" to be on, I discovered it.

Influence

By and large, I believe that the people of the United States of America have mostly forgotten the experience of God: we remember the name, but not the face. We have begun to confuse the menu for the meal and grow ever more hungry, fighting each other over how to properly order, while back in the kitchen tables groan under the weight of the food prepared for the feast of feasts. Folks aren't even ordering, let alone eating! I feel that a significant part of the unfed spiritual hunger that many experience has to do with menu confusion. We spend so much time squabbling over quibbles with the text that we never get around to experiencing the nourishment to which the menu refers. Put another way, I think that the language we use to describe God greatly influences our perspective and experience means of access to the Divine. When we fight pettily among ourselves, our religion can come to *feel* petty. We end up not liking the restaurant because of the horrific fight we had with one another before even getting to taste the meal. It is through this lens that I have come to the field of theopoetics.

I understand theopoetics to be the theory and practice of making God known in the world. I have arrived at this definition, at least partially, by means of the word's etomology. *Theos*, the Greek for God, most of us are familiar with. Poetics, though, has a less well-known origin. The word *poiein* in Greek is a verb meaning "to make or shape." At a root level then, theopoetics is how we make God, how God comes to be known by us, and academically, the study of the ways in which God is made known through texts. What I have discovered, less by etymology and more by experience, is that words we encounter that articulate ways of being for the Divine and the Divinely inspired are with us far beyond their life on the page. That is to say, while theopoetics may be construed as a primarily monograph-based discipline and a child of the Literary Theory movement, I think there is more life in understanding it as a means to grapple broadly with how we speak of God, the ways in which we articulate the numinious, and the shades of God-claims to which we are continually exposed throughout religious dialogue and supposedly secular forms of media.

As the religious content of sermon and church conversation is usually self-evident, it behooves us to be aware of the messages we recieve from other sources as well. A theopoet isn't just writing god-talk in verse, she is articulating the depths of reality with such expressive precision that the omnipresent nature of the Divine is seen, by those with eyes to see, in the text. There is a universality to this type of writing which I hesitate to categorize as solely religious. As T.S. Eliot wrote, there are "great religious poets, but they are, by comparison with Dante, specialists. That is all they can do. And Dante, because he could do everything else, is for that reason the greatest "religious" poet, though to call him a "religious poet" would be to abate his universality.[5] "In the same expansive spirit that claims Dante as a universal "religious poet," I am interested in cultivating the capacity of universal "religious poetry readers," so skilled in their craft that they are capable of experiencing the Presence in a reading of the world that continues daily and unabated.

From the shoulder-riding devil and angel of Warner Brothers cartoons, to the continued proclamaition of a just, God-supported war, media-consuming North Americans are continuously exposed to myriad messages on the nature of Divinity and how it appears in the world. I am captivated by the notion that we can make explicit the nature of these media, and the ways by which we subsequently come to think about the Divine and express our experience of the Sacred. Through the development of a critical awareness, we begin to become awake to the ubiquity of theological thinking, even in places where we would not expect it. Moreover, beyond the mere awareness of "theological thinking," we also grow in our capacity to sense that of God in the world: I believe that the language we use to describe God greatly affects our perspective and perception of the Divine. I feel met in these convictions by the field of theopoetics, which takes seriously the possibility that the messages we receive *about* God can alter our experience *of* God. This is not to suggest that the Divine itself is directly altered by a Bugs Bunny animation arguing with a pitchfork-wielding devil, but rather that as creatures of media, words, images, and stories continue to influence us long after we hear Porky proclaim "Th-Th-Th-That's all, folks."

Fuchsia

During the course of my travels, I discovered the reason I had had my flight diverted several times, the reason I had had the pleasure of being exposed to my very own Magic Fingers bed, and the reason why my interview had to be rescheduled three times. Finally, *en route* to Rochester, I had a vivid dream in which I saw that I would minister to a woman who would be waiting for me at the Rochester airport. Waiting that morning at exactly the time I arrived, not the day before. I woke with a clear image of this woman's face. She was in her late fifties and had an olive complexion and graying brunette curls worn close to her shoulder so that they brushed the top of a once-bright fucsia scarf. She was having a panic attack and calling repeatedly for a priest, and when no priest was to be found, I stepped forward. There I was able to pray with her and bring her some measure of comfort as she readied to fly to the funeral of her son. Sometimes things happen that we cannot predict.

That was the dream at least.

When I arrived in reality, having deplaned certain of this woman's presence, I exited only to be met by the thundering roar of the everyday. No fucsia scarf, no son's funeral, not even a woman. The early morning airport was nearly empty, and I was able to walk from my gate to the nearest coffee vendor without running into a single person. I was shocked. I had been so sure that she would be there.

Revelation

Even the stories we create for ourselves are powerful.

In many ways, I understand theopoetics, à la McLuhan, to be a type of theology-less theological expression. Another way to approach this is to consider the degree to which the formal work of theology is carried out by means of postulation and abstraction. The presentation of theopoetics, while covering the same ground, tends to travel that ground in a different way. By emphasizing communication and expression, theopoetics encourages the drawing forth of actual experiences of God in the world and an attempt to articulate how it is that the Divine has manifested. While Scripture certainly contains myriad instances of God in the world, often people want to know how it is that god is now, in these days, and how we can speak of the Divine and god's work.

In the book *The Power of Myth*,[6] a remarkable series of conversations are captured between journalist Bill Moyers and mythologist Joseph Campbell. During the course of one of those conversations, Campbell remarks that clergy are not concerned enough with the connotations of symbols and are instead overly focused on pragmatic ethicism. Asked by Moyers why this might be the case, he replies as follows:

> The difference between a priest and a shaman is that the priest is a functionary and the shaman is someone who has had an experience. In our tradition [Catholicism] it is the monk who seeks the experience, while the priest is the one who has studied to serve the community.
>
> I had a friend who attended an international meeting of the Roman Catholic meditative orders, which was held in Bangkok. He told me that the Catholic monks had no problems understanding the Buddhist monks, but that it was the clergy of the two religions who were unable to understand each other.
>
> The person who has had a mystical experience knows that all the symbolic expressions of it are faulty. The symbols don't render the experience, they suggest it. If you haven't had the experience, how can you know what it is? Try to explain the joy of skiing to somebody living in the tropics who has never even seen snow. There has to be an experience to catch the message, some clue—otherwise you're not hearing what is being said (73).

In his response, Moyers remarks that "the person who has the experience has to project it in the best way he/she can with images, [and] it seems to me that we have lost the art in our society of thinking images (73)." Amos Wilder, one of the early proponents of theopoetics, would have agreed with this completely. In the opening passages of his book *Theopoetic*,[7] he offers that his "plea for a theopoetic means doing more justice to the symbolic and the pre-rational in the way we deal with experience. We should recognize that human nature and human societies are more deeply motivated by images and fabulations than by ideas" (2).

Theopoetics places an emphasis on the descriptive and minimizes the prescriptive. It is a means of linguistically re-engaging and re-envisioning the world and the ways in which we percieve God to be agentive within it. When a text is acting theopoetically, it functions in opposing directions, simultaneously pulling the reader further into the text's poetic narrative and pushing the reader into a reconsideration of, and reconnection with, life in the world beyond the text.[8] The theopoet is less concerned with correctly arguing the nature of reality and more with expressing how the Divine is sometimes revealed through it.

Vineyard

In 1812, the American ornithologist John James Audubon painted the first image of a bird flying. It was a whippoorwill. The occasion of this painting is notable because in it Audubon broke with standards of period ornithological illustration. To more "properly" depict the nature and action of the bird in flight in three-dimensional space, he used artistic techniques of foreshortening; the nearest parts of the bird were enlarged so that the rest of the form appeared to have depth and go back into the space of the painting. Because of this foreshortening, accurate measurements could not be taken from the illustration. Audubon painted things "incorrectly" to capture their movement and aid in their identification. As a result, some his images lost their merit as scientific tools.[9]

I have come to believe that the issue is not so much that speaking of the Divine is impossible, but rather that it is impossible to speak about with objective certainty. At best, theology becomes less relevant the more the theologian employs solely the language of logic. At worst, it can become an exercise of tilting-at-windmills, attempting to enumerate the single-way things are and always will be. And this problem exists outside of the academic walls of seminary and divinity school as well.

If a young child is taught her creative painting is wrong, or not performed properly, it is likely that she will eventually withdraw from painting, regardless of how nonsensical the teachings may be. Those in positions of power contribute a significant amount to what it is we think is acceptable and what is off limits. It seems to me that the current situation of popular theology is not that dissimilar. At some level, people appear to be afraid of trying to talk about God and getting it wrong.[10]

Many people, both within my tradition and elsewhere, struggle to find language to articulate their sense of the Divine. There are a variety of reasons why this can be the case; however, the end product is that there are a number of people in the contemporary culture who are not fully comfortable with the formal dogmatic positions of their own denomination of origin and do not feel as if the proposed theology of the tradition matches their experience of God in the world. Unfortunately, people also often feel equally uncomfortable questioning these positions from within the institution. Questioning is often discouraged, and literalism and/or adherence to tradition becomes the order of the day. A regrettable consequence of this dynamic is that some choose to remain within their tradition, their own voice silenced, and others choose to leave, only voicing their concerns from without. In both situations, an opportunity for dialogue is missed, and in so missing, another possibility to enrich the conversation of the Church has been lost.

The danger of valuing experience so highly is that people might come to believe that their own experience trumps all else. Often conservative critics of theopoetic and expressive thinking claim that it is bound to end up in some kind of relativistic, solipsistic hedonism. *Who cares about tradition? Let's do what feels good, what I experience as good for me is good!* While this position is extreme, it represents a misunderstanding of what I believe the theopoetic invitation to be. I do not see theopoetics as a destructive discipline replacing theology. Theopoetics is a way of perceiving and expressing experience so as to more directly articulate how the Divine manifests in the world. It presumes that there is some life-giving Source to creativity and creation, and that at times it is more noticed than others. I am not interested in attempting to disprove theological tenets; in fact, it seems to me that theopoetics is related to theology much the way that a vineyard is related to a horticultural museum. Both are of service, and of interest, to different populations at different times, and not in conflict with each other.

Audubon did not seek the destruction of images from which measurements could be taken, *and* he knew that he could offer something more.

Ground
After talking with me about theopoetics, people are often left with the impression that language occupies a space in my life that borders on the obsessive. I don't reject this out of hand, but it does bring to mind an interview with Stanley Kunitz I once read.

In it, he evokes William Blake in asserting that he succeeds as a poet only as much as he is capable of evincing the "minute particulars" of a situation. The specificity of corporeal experience is essential to Kunitz. He comments that "it is an advantage for the poet not always to be immersed in poetry, not to become incestuous with his own art... [Too] much poetry is airy. It is spun only out of the need to write the poem and is not nailed into the foundations of the life itself."[11] The retreat of his garden was a place wherein he could come to literal grips with that life. He fended off obsession with poetry by immersing himself in the "minute particulars" of his flower beds. So it's not that I don't love language—I do—it's that language is my garden.

It is in its tended rows that I find enough expression of the everyday to hedge against a type of airy theorizing and abstract theology that I hope to avoid. It is precisely because of my love of the Divine that I find myself drawn to text with a passion. It refreshes me and returns me to my own ground. Consequently, I try to tend to it as best I can, aware of its limitations and all the more careful because of them given how much I ask it to produce. I do not want to overtax the soil.

I do not view language deterministically. While it is powerful, it is neither omnipotent nor a full substitute for the experiences of life. It surely influences our human sense of things, and I firmly believe that it works in concert with our cultural context to evoke all manner of emotional and intimate responses, yet I balk at claiming that words can inherently exert control over anything. While poetries are indeed enchanting they are not magic. The power of song and prose is part and parcel of the creative impulse of Spirit, not its precursor.

By exploring within the relatively fixed media of language, we attune our sensibilities to more readily interpret reality through the lens of our faith rather than that of the dominant culture. The more we practice seeing God, the easier the task becomes. Will we ever be able to see the whole of Divinity continuously? If Moses' experience on Mount Sinai was any indication, no. This doesn't mean, though, that the task isn't worth attempting in part. I see the inward work of religion as continuous rather than discrete. I understand the cultivation of a Spirit-led life to be a process, not an instant of conversion. While Grace is received, and many Sauls have been turned *en route* to Damascus, I am more interested in the path on which Saul placed his feet after conversion than the place where he fell to the earth.

I believe that part of the rise of theopoetic perspectives will be a parallel call to dialogue and communal connection. Engaging in the theopoetic process means coming to terms with the Gracious Presence that unites all things, even in this broken world. It means learning to perceive Spirit at work in the mundane and transcending modern alienation with a call to unite and serve. Just as Kunitz gained recognition through his poetry though it was his garden that fed him, so too do we come to know one another through words and actions although it is that deeper, quiet place of God that unites us. So as not to become engaged in infinite navel-gazing and/or personal obliteration in the face of constant direct divinity, we can choose to create language that captures shades of that experience in such a way that others recognize it and are affected by it. In some cases, affection is the effect, and those affected are "lavishly flung forth"[12] into the world where they encounter others and inspire other work. At best, theopoetics is a means of engaging language, and perception in such a way that one enters into a radical relation with the Divine, the Other, and the Creation in which all occurs.

Dance
Scott Holland has written that theopoetics "is a kind of writing that invites more writing. Its narratives lead to other narratives, its metaphors encourage new metaphors, its confessions invoke more confessions, and its conversations invite more conversations,"[13] and while I agree with this statement, I find it akin to defining love by saying that "it is a kind of emotion." It is true, and yet it does not capture the fullness. Theopoetics is a type of writing, *and* I would like to offer that it is a way of perceiving as well. The theopoet as wordsmith can so craft because she sees theopoetically, because she is looking for all the ways her experiences are variations on a Divine theme. Her poems then, or prose, or songs, are new iterations and utterances of that eternal Word which was in the beginning. Is she crafting new scripture? No, not as such, but she has served to manifest another means by which we may more fully come to know the movement of the Spirit.

Is her service needed? Strictly speaking, probably not. Every moment is, in and of itself, inherently a possible gateway into a deepening life of faith; Grace is available and abundant regardless of what we do. This, of course, begs the question: What is the point of it then? Why bother writing? To proceed down this path asks us to consider the possibility that any human-initiated act is superfluous. Given the saturation of Divinity throughout our experience, there is no need for additional contributions. God's got it covered.

If some choose the above path, I will not begrudge them, but I for one find the argument a bloodless and abstracted one that leaves little room for the reality of human proclivity and failing. Do I want to encourage human frailty? Not at all, but I do want to be honest in acknowledging that often we don't percieve the Divine, that we are enfleshed, that we sometimes do need to be jolted out of various stupors, and that there is joy in song and dance and play. These acknowledgments are core to my understanding of the field: a theopoetic perspective is one that admits an element of playfulness, joy, and grit into a project interested in putting words to the numinous. It is a corrective to abstraction that has no experiential grounding and, like art, is bound intimately within the context of our community. While the artist can declare his work as peerless, ultimately it is community and time that determine the profundity of a piece.

I am not asking that we accept every voice as truth. I am asking that we make room for every voice to be heard, with an understanding that everyone has something to offer. To paraphrase Holland, theopoetics is an invitation and its response: narratives, metaphors, confessions, and conversations all spiraling around and through that which is true. It is a dance and a blossoming, a longing and a love affair.

Field

In a footnote to his essay "U.S. Hispanic Popular Catholicism as Theopoetics," Roberto Goizueta makes a gripping claim that pertains directly to theopoetics.

> The existence of its "unity and rootedness in praxis preclude the possibility of a theopoetics immune to theological and ethical critique. There can be no apolitical or a-theological affect any

more than there can be an apolitical or affectless theology; the most sterile logic cannot be completely devoid of affect any more than a mind can exist without a body. A theopoetics that sets itself over against theology and ethics distorts human praxis and, thus, expresses a distorted view of the God revealed in that praxis."[14]

In this text, I see an articulation of theopoetics as a resonating process set to oscillation by simultaneous forces of esthetics, ethics, experience, and reason. I find great hope in this admission of theopoetics as a field of inquiry somewhat apart from the specialized disciplines of formal academia. It is related by means of abstracted critical study, poetics, and artistic vision and yet is also grounded in an engagement with the political and social world. It suggests that just as humans are complex creatures with many facets and means of participating in humanity, perhaps there is a way of communicating and partaking in spiritual experience in such a way that is more inclusive of multiple modalities.

Goizueta's articulation is appealing to me because it takes into consideration various facets of the human experience and sets them in motion around the centrality of God, allowing for diversity of expression. I think about it like a gyroscope, whose massive moving center is the means by which the object as whole can be kept upright. Our tendency, where God is concerned, is to overemphasize a particular quality of divinity at the exclusion of other aspects in what I understand as a misguided attempt to name and claim God. The result is an off-balanced worldview in every sense of the German *Weltanschauung*. When certain modalities, such as rational scientific prose, rise to cultural dominance, even in fields better suited to other means of connection, such as religion, the result is that any engagement with the material in question is irrevocably altered by the means used to engage it.

While it may well bear equal part insolence and audacity, it strikes me that the point in question here might best be illustrated by amending the contents of one of Rumi's most quoted poems. I tamper with his verse in the hope that my short poetic intrusion will serve better than a page of prose, and, in the event of offense, that it can be forgiven once carried out.

Out beyond ideas of wrongdoing and rightdoing,
                beauty and disgust,
                I, you, and them,
                and fantasy and fact,
there is a field. I will meet you there.
When the soul lies down in that grass,
the world is too full to talk about
                using the cutting words we have learned in school.
Ideas, language, even the phrase "each other"
doesn't make any sense.
                So let us not speak but sing
                and in the singing share
                that which cannot be spoken.

Call

At the end of the day, I hope that by working with language in an integrative and expansive way, we find another tool to open ourselves up to experiences that are themselves ever expanding and integrating. I feel that the liberating quality of Art is a learned experience, and once we have developed the means to perceive it as such, we can more regularly enter into moments of freedom in all areas of our life. Once we have developed a taste for a certain type of fruit or poem, we come to appreciate its nuances and sweetness all the more. This, it seems to me, traces the same path as discipleship.

    Mere association with Jesus was not sufficient for the disciples to understand the gospel that he brought. As we read in Mark 9:32, "They understood not his sayings and were afraid to ask him." Although ignorant at times, they could serve and feel some great measure of comfort without being alienated or ridiculed by Jesus. The same is available to us: we can proceed in service, afraid to ask questions and yet still be of Divine use. And yet, is not some measure of connectedness lost when we remain confused? I am not suggesting it is necessary or possible to understand the full power and process of God. I do feel, though, that a fuller sense of the Great Work is available.

In John 15:15, Jesus reminds the disciples that they are to be called friends because friends can know the Lord's reasoning, while servants merely serve. Perhaps, the presence of the Gospel is enough alone, but in my foolishness and exuberance, I want not just to hear it but to experience it as Spirit breaks anew into my life and brings some measure of creative refreshment. I want to find ways to express how it is that I am inspired and I want to hear how it is that others experience the Divine. In that conversation, I cannot help but feel that I find an easier path into fellowship and a greater sense of understanding: the power of the Gospel is not just in text on the page, but in that text as it is given breath in the lives and actions of the human communities committed to each other and to the work of the Kingdom. To better understand this text, and each other, I think we can continue to develop ways of speaking to one another that help to clarify our experience of God in the world and guide us toward the truth of what we are called to as a people.

And while we might never discern the whole of that truth, we might as well seek some measure of it. In so doing perhaps we will find new ways that the Gospel can speak to us and through us. To this point, Peter Rollins has performed an amazing job of articulating this sense of communal truth-seeking. He writes that religious truth shouldn't be considered fact in the way we scientifically use the word. He asks us to consider religious truth not as a means of defining reality, but as way of transforming reality. When we do this, he suggests that "instead of truth being an epistemological description, it is rediscovered as a soteriological event (an event that brings healing and salvation). This is no more a form of relativism than it is a form of absolutism; rather, it is an understanding of truth as that which transforms us into more Christ-like individuals."[15]

My sense is that liberating discipleship is a process best explored in expressive community. Within the context of that body, we can test our personal experience against that of others, developing skills of discernment and articulation in the journey toward an understanding of what it is we are called to in this world. And while I have no clear, direct sense of an ultimate reality, I find that I can concur with the poet Louise Glück. "Whatever the truth is, to speak it is a great adventure.[16]

Discovery

And so while I didn't meet my mystery woman there in the Rochester airport, I did meet God. There in the empty, expectant space, the potential for anything to happen was opened up. I was prepared to be yolked into service and was willing to be transformed in the experience. The specifics of my dreams were not seen, but for following them I found reward. In the early quiet of that western New York morning I came to be grateful again for having stories that I can believe, and for living a life in which I have the chance to believe them. The in-breaking of Spirit is profound and the pregnancy which marks those moments of revelation is Divine indeed.

> My God is the god in the next room,
> cooking unseen feasts and humming;
>
> the ache of the moment before the rain
> when you're sure the whole June
> cloud is ready to burst through
> though you haven't felt single drop;
>
> the photographer's ironic smile
> after her darkroom discovery
> that in the background of a misfire
> she has captured two lovers gazing
> longingly at each other's meals;
>
> the dandelion blade that insists
> adamantly that it must reside directly
> in the middle of your neighbor's
> suburban blacktopped driveway;
>
> the sight of the shadow of a bird flitting
> by the sill near the bed of an aging Grace,
> who can no longer move but counts herself
> lucky because at least she can still see.
>
> This is my God:
>   expectant and grinning,
>   wild and near.[17]

Notes

1. McLuhan, Eric. "Marshall McLuhan's theory of communication: The Yegg." *Global Media Journal — Canadian Edition, 1.1 (2008):* 25–43.
2. Keefe-Perry, L. B. C. "Theopoetics: Process and Perspective." *Christianity and Literature.* 58.4 (2009).
3. McLuhan, Eric. "Marshall McLuhan's theory of communication: The Yegg." *Global Media Journal — Canadian Edition*, 1.1 (2008): 26.
4. McLuhan, Marshall. "Casting My Perils Before Swains" *McLuhan: Hot & Cool.* Ed. Gerald Emanuel Stearn. New York: Signet Books, 1969. xii.
5. Eliot, Thomas S. *To Criticize the Critic and Other Writings.* New York: Farrar, Straus & Giroux, 1965, 134. Also cited in Eric McLuhan's piece.
6. Campbell, Joseph, and Bill Moyers. *The Power of Myth.* New York: Anchor Printing, 1991, 73.
7. Wilder, Amos N. *Theopoetic: Theology and the Religious Imagination.* Philadelphia: Fortress Press, 1976, 2.
8. Keefe-Perry, L. B. C. "Theopoetics: Process and Perspective." *Christianity and Literature.* 58.4 (2009): 592.
9. Bierregaard, Richard O. "John James Audubon—A Bird's-eye View." The Department of Biology University of North Carolina at Charlotte. Accessed August 24, 2009 at http://www.bioweb.uncc.edu/bierregaard/audubon.htm.
10. I do not intend to include here those that compose what is often referred to as the "New Atheists." I do not believe they are afraid. They are worth considering briefly, though, so as to hold them in relief to those uncomfortable with voicing their personal sense. I often find that atheistic arguments against God articulate a host of qualities which I too challenge. As it pertains to this piece, the relevant item is that all atheistic arguments I have come across have as fixed an idea of God as do literal, fundamentalist theologians. While they might take separate sides in the debate, both believe they are arguing from firm and fixed ground. So whether it be atheism or "protheism," those who encounter mystery and do not presume to force it to conform are surrounded on all sides by people telling them that God is indeed one certain way.
11. Luphor, David. "Language Surprised." *Interviews and Encounters with Stanley Kunitz.* Ed. Stanley Moss. Riverdale-on-Hudson, NY: Sheep Meadow, 1993, 6.
12. Rilke, Rainer M. "Poem II, 26." *Rilke's Book of Hours: Love Poems to God.* Trans. Anita Barrows and Joanna Macy. Riverhead Trade, 2005, 122.
13. Holland, Scott. "Theology Is a Kind of Writing: The Emergence of Theopoetics." *Cross Currents* 47.3 (1997): 317–331.
14. Goizueta, Roberto S. "U.S. Hispanic Popular Catholicism as Theopoetics." *Hispanic/Latino Theology: Challenge and Promise.* Eds. Ada María Isasi-Díaz and Fernando F. Segovia. Minneapolis: Fortress, 1996, 264.
15. Rollins, Peter. "Christian A/Theism." *Movement: Termly Magazine of the Student Christian Movement.* 122 (2006): 15.
16. Glück, Louise. "To My Teacher." *Interviews and Encounters with Stanley Kunitz.* Ed. Stanley Moss. Riverdale-on-Hudson, NY: Sheep Meadow, 1993. 140.
17. Keefe-Perry, L. B. C. "Bird Shadows," *Spirit Rising.* Ed. Angelina Conti, et al. Quakers Uniting in Publications (QUIP), forthcoming.

THEOPOETICS AND SOCIAL CHANGE

Matt Guynn

> We open up the hungers and longings of our age. We enter into a conversation with the deepest places of our selves and our audience. To engage in the theopoetic is to tempt the radical nature of ourselves, it is to follow in the footsteps of the God-Speakers that could upset the republic, could speak from the margins of our hungers and unspeakable truths.
>
> Jason Derr, *In Consideration of the Theopoetic*[1]

What is the activity of a priestess of the social imagination? What focus shall a theopoetic social change agent take? How can we as social change organizers both "upset the republic," in Derr's language, and also awaken the hungers and strengths of the human heart, accessing the power and Presence of imagination and of God-Deity-Divinity-Mystery? This essay is a report from the field, an update about ways that theopoetic intent has informed one set of experiments in social change organizing.

The theopoet argues that, in many cases, like old soda pop, language has gone flat in our religious traditions. We use the same language again and again without examining and refreshing it, and often no one really wants to drink it any longer. Bound up with the flatness of language, our rituals become rote. Instead of actually interacting with Deity-Divinity-Essence-God, rituals and religious conversation become routinized. Rather than paths of power, we tread paths of habit.[2]

In *Theopoetic: Theology and the Religious Imagination,* Amos Wilder asserted that when language gets too encrusted, it fails to produce either new theophanies or Spirit-fed enactments of ancient truth. The conversation in which Wilder participated, with artists, musicians, mystics, and psychologists, was about the integration of soul into spirit, the re-introduction of ecstasy into religion, the renewed embrace of vision/hymn/poem as categories of God-talk.[3]

There is a risk that theopoetics will remain just a conversation corner in the academy: Yes, the writing may evoke more writing, but these rivers of words deserve to also flow into the sanctuary and toward the streets. If theopoetics is to keep growing toward its real promise of more powerful engagements with Mystery-Absence-God-Presence, then theopoetics will need to find life not only in the pages of journals, but also in worship services that midwife the new/ancient humanity, and in incarnate experiments of struggles for justice/peace. The latter is the focus of this essay.

Theopoetics as a stance promises to deepen and develop social change organizing, by enriching issue-based organizing with a search for an empowerment rooted in Presence and Power. The theopoetic activist wants not just words—but enfleshed initiative. The theopoet change-maker seeks new re-engagements of faith stories. Not only community change, but individual regeneration. And not only individual salvations, but full-bodied wholeness, for the person, the faith community, the neighborhood. The theopoet leader is a change agent who speaks not just in slogan and catchphrase, but from the currents of a deeper Life.

I am concerned that many times, those of us in spiritual social change leadership fall short of the mark. Too often, it is possible to fall into the kinds of patterns that theopoetics train us to be skeptical about—for example, to fall into the rhetorical trap of using the same tired constructions of Us vs. Them, instead of seeking new framings that catalyze the imagination and spirit in the direction of hopeful action. And it is far too easy for faith-based leaders to retell scripture stories only to make moral points about justice or peace, but not to dwell in them with their people, to access power in new/ancient ways. Far too easy to continue to plan the same old vigil, the same kinds of rote civil disobedience, which become themselves a kind of tired and flat language that no one hears anymore.

I have at times taken these easier roads. But I am hungry, and I think I join many others in my yearning, for faith-rooted social change activism which draws from wells the run from a deeper Source, and achieves fresh and generative political relevance. I want to learn a kind of social change that both organizes around specific initiatives and accompanies people and communities into a new kind of visionary leadership and spiritual/community power.

I am practicing a leadership that bridges toward vision and community-building, and an ever-clearer practice for empowerment of specific communities with which I work. Those particularly in my mind as I write these reflections are other social change organizers and community leaders who are discovering/seeking how we might organize by helping foster dreams and a sense of the possible.

There is a longing for imagination and possibility, sometimes buried under the mountains of facts, failures, realities, and conclusions. For all those interested in social ferment and social change—this *imagination*, rooted in transcendence, issuing forth new glimpses of the Divine Possibility, is the gold for which we mine, the water for which we tremblingly hold a divining rod in our hands.

How is imagination awakened? The smell of a lilac bush wafting on air; a refrain from an old song; the sight of a childhood home. The words of a sermon, the voice of a friend, the touch of a lover. The hint of things not yet ripe, but ripening. Flashes of bright color. Time alone or in community. Silence. Memory.[4]

How is imagination awakened for renewing a community, renewing our world? Much the same way: Hints and curling questions, hopes held out, along with bridges to hopeful action.

My main context for experiments in theopoetics and social change is my congregational peace and justice organizing as part of the staff of On Earth Peace, a US-based ministry rooted in the Church of the Brethren.[5] This work has included support calls for peace-committed congregations in the months following 9/11; equipping congregational initiatives around the country related to alternatives to the military and counter-recruitment, and undergirding congregational ministries for military returning from Iraq and Afghanistan. Because of time I have spent soaking in the waters of constructive theology and theopoetics, I bring those perspectives to this congregational work.[6]

I came into my early efforts committed to meet people where they were and explore what was really happening with them. I wanted to connect in a "seedly" or "gardenish" manner with the people I was contacting—connecting in a deeper way, understanding the forces they were up against and the specific situations they encountered.

I wanted to be a theopoetic social change organizer, not "just" organizing around specific initiatives, but using my efforts as an organizer to create spaces for people's political and spiritual power to emerge more fully. Not reiterating slogans and statements, but tilling the soil so that new life could emerge.

I will focus on three parts of On Earth Peace's work that have involved aspects of the theopoetic: theological reflection with organizers, one-on-one support calls, and our annual campaign surrounding the International Day of Prayer for Peace. In each of these, a theopoetic sensibility enters in through the awakening of imagination about self, social change work and its possibilities, and Source.

Theological reflection with social change organizers

In the ramping-up period of the wars in Iraq and Afghanistan, communities we were connected with were experiencing a heightened or more visible pressure and presence from military recruiters seeking to fill their recruitment goals. People across the country began (or continued existing efforts) to speak up—sometimes confronting the recruiters—and sometimes seeking to address the root causes of the situation (such as a lack of opportunity for young people).[7] In response to a swelling number of requests, On Earth Peace offered bimonthly networking phone calls for congregationally based organizers responding to military recruitment and generating alternatives for youth in their communities.

A typical call connected people from coast to coast in the United States, and included theological reflection, open sharing time, and strategy.[8] The theological reflections were spacious, poetic homilies, with time for meditation and sharing. They were intended to foster communal reflection on our work in light of the stories of scripture and the activity of God. Here is one example, on demons, disease, and counter-recruitment organizing.

Luke 9

> From Luke 9 (NRSV): *1 When Jesus had called the Twelve together, he gave them power and authority to drive out all demons and to cure diseases, 2 and he sent them out to preach the kingdom of God and to heal the sick.*

Jesus sends us out as people in the Way, getting in the Way, to drive out demons and cure diseases, preaching the kingdom of God and healing the sick. Too often, a contemporary hearing of words like "demon" and "disease" can *either* focus only on special powers that the early church had—thereby proving its God-touched uniqueness which is inaccessible to us—*or* dismiss it as fable.

As we prepare ourselves to be sent out as counter-recruiters in the fullness of God's power, it matters for us to be empowered by these words, for we are not "just" political agitators. We are not "just" naysayers concerned about specific foreign policy choices.

Our commission is a deeper one than that to grapple with demon and disease, to preach the kingdom, and to heal the sick.

What might demon mean here? For me, personally: despair, isolation, depression, the weight of the world's broken beauty. Reflect silently: *What demons or diseases do you struggle with?*

I often feel too weak, or too afflicted, by my own demons and diseases to go out and heal others. Sometimes, I am tempted to heal and cast out of others that which is still binding me.

But the strange and silent presence of Jesus liberates us, or promises to, as we draw close. What if we, in preparation for counter-recruitment, drew close to receive our own healing?

What demons and diseases might our communities face? Apathy, materialism, racism, economic blight, an addiction to revenge, a blindness which prevents even seeing the other parts of one's own community. *What demons or disease might your own community be facing? (Call them out.)*

The path toward the Way, toward a counter-recruitment organizing of *spirit and power*, will involve in a neverending spiral *both* our own deep spiritual and psychological healing *and* our stepping forward with spiritual power to cast out demons.

Counter-recruitment can preach about and reach for shalom communities,

where demons of racism and empire and self-hatred are cast out,

where each one is loosed of the bonds that restrain them,

where economic blight is healed to become the flourishing thriving of justice and right,

where blindness is replaced by joyful sight.

God, meet us in our need. Give us vision to see and name the spiritual diseases that are making us sick. Cast out demons that bind us and our communities. Give us the wisdom to see and engage the work that is before us, in all its dimensions. AMEN.[9]

One-on-one support calls for organizers

A main way that On Earth Peace organizers have connected with congregationally based peace and justice organizers around the country is on the phone. These one-on-one calls offer support to different people on different issues, with a continuing intent to awaken imagination and connect to deeper resources.

At their best, three main things happen in each call: coaching, connection to broader movements, and spiritual accompaniment. By coaching, I mean helping people look at their organizing through a lens of strategy and eliciting their thoughts about allies, obstacles, resources, and what victory might look like in concrete terms. Connection to broader movements means providing stories and information from specific relevant movements and providing affirmation for participating in the river of non-violent social change.

Spiritual accompaniment in this context has several aspects:
- Acknowledging and opening to spiritual power
- Praying for the person before the call
- Praying with the person on the call
- Connecting to scripture story, and the story of God's love
- Asking, How is God moving in you through this work? What is happening in your heart and spirit?

- Asking, how is this part of what God is doing in the world?
- Acknowledging the forbidden, the dark side, and harder aspects of the work

The heart of each call is to nurture the individual's leadership as a faith-based peacemaker and their congregation's/community's leadership as an influence for long-term change. The calls are meant to be pastoral in tending to the heart of the organizers, and prophetic in asking questions about next steps.

The main technique is the elicitive question: not *telling*, but asking, inviting their story and their dreams to come out. This elicitive approach reflects the heart of the theopoetic commitment.[10]

Organizing for the International Day of Prayer for Peace and beyond

In 2007, On Earth Peace started organizing around the International Day of Prayer for Peace. Each year, September 21 is both the World Council of Churches' International Day of Prayer for Peace and the United Nations' International Day of Peace. On or near September 21, 2009, a total of 148 congregations and community groups who connected with On Earth Peace led events in their community.

In these efforts, we use a questioning and imagination-awakening approach. The core catalyzing question is, "What's the violence that's impacting your community?" We ask congregations to wrestle with that question and to begin taking that question and related questions out into their community. "What do we need to know, if we want to care about what's happening here? What are the ways that people's lives are less than they could be, here in our community? What are the signs of hope? What might God be doing with our community right now?"[11]

The intention is that these questions, and this engagement, lead congregations into new relationships, and into new understandings of their community, so that when the community is gathered on September 21 for a public prayer event, a new thing will happen—some new coalescence, some new foundation for a next step in creative public action on the community's pressing issues.

To support this, we offer an organizing manual and training calls on topics including (1) how to lead a community listening initiative; (2) principles of non-violence leadership for community change; (3) media outreach and coverage; and (4) planning a public prayer service that people will turn out for. These training calls supplement a series of about six one-on-one support calls that we offer to congregational organizers leading up to September 21.

In the end, we are not just interested in what happens on September 21. We are interested in people and communities that grow in their leadership, and have informed perspectives, and are rooted in prayer and ready to move their communities toward justice and non-violence. The IDOPP campaign was also about changing notions of peacemaking—from anti-negative, to a positive and proactive peacemaking. We want to form and spiritually accompany people, not just fill their heads with ideas about peacemaking. This is why a question-raising model, in which we walk with the individuals through their struggles with engagement, matters so much. We are interested in the deeper spiritual formation, in the people who emerge from our interactions.

One of the ways that we followed up September 21, 2008, was a training event called "You Can't Stop the River: Community Change for Congregations." Ministry teams gathered from congregations from around the country that were ready to take action on a specific issue in their community. About ten congregations came together in Kansas City, Kansas, in April 2009, to work on issues ranging from hungry children in the community, to gun violence, to recruitment of youth by drug dealers.

The retreat incorporated training on effective non-violence leadership along with theology and scripture, prayer and inspiration. We worked to awaken the imagination of the people who were there, and also equip them, so that when they got home, they could develop a process in their own community that would enliven, involve, and accomplish specific goals. The event included prayer time, together and alone; worship and healing services, as well as engagement with scripture and each other and the heritage of non-violent community change.

Growing the seeds is ultimately not our work
Meister Eckhart wrote: "The seed of God is in us. Given an intelligent and hard-working farmer, it will thrive and grow up to God, whose seed it is; and accordingly its fruits will be God-nature. Pear seeds grow into pear trees, nut seeds into nut trees, and God-seed into God."[12]

As we discussed these matters, my friend Carol Carson responded: "The organizer is the farmer, and if you want to follow Eckhart, God has planted the seed. The seed still has the responsibility to grow. You can't make it grow. No matter what a farmer does, she cannot make a seed grow. She can do everything possible to create the right environment to allow the seed to reach its potential."[13]

Theopoetic social change organizing is about nurturing seeds of God—seeds of personality, of justice, of beauty, and of right relationship. This is the work of a Lover, a Beloved, a Gardener, a Builder. The theopoet seeks to support, undergird, and bless the seed within those she organizes, but ultimately the seed itself is what grows, guided and directed by the imprint/image within.

Theopoetic social change seeks the power of deeper making and creativity—and seeks to unleash it from within the communities and individuals where it abides. Theopoetic social change seeks the Word made flesh—the enfleshment of visions and Power within the realities of the people each theopoet loves and relates to. When it moves from page to sanctuary and streets, theopoetics will provoke a creative collision of poem and picket, a fertile pollination of Art and Presence, a restless longing for the Life within and beyond the Absence.

Theopoetic activists are called to tend to the heart and the imagination and the spiritual power of people and communities. This is the heart of theopoetic social change—unlocking personal-power-from-within, engaging myth and theology in new ways, walking with people while they develop the programs and initiatives that are rooted in engagement with God and deeply relevant to their own situations. Elicitive, but not just elicitive for its own sake, a theopoetic of social change carefully moves toward spiritual power, toward initiatives and experiments that are not just theory, but which take concrete form, that take flesh and have body.

Notes

1. Article accessed on August 30, 2009, at http://www.zimbio.com/Theopoetic/articles/6/Consideration+Theopoetic.
2. For a summary of the state of the conversation on theopoetics, I commend you to L. B. C. Keefe-Perry, "Theopoetics: Process and Perspective," *Christianity and Literature*, Vol. 58, No. 4 (Summer 2009).
3. Minneapolis: Fortress Press, 1976.

4. Rubem Alves' beautiful meditation on Christology, memory and imagination, *I Believe in the Resurrection of the Body* (Eugene, OR: Wipf and Stock Publishers, 2003), begins with memories provoked by the scent of a lilac bush.
5. Please visit http://www.onearthpeace.org.
6. My MA thesis was *Re-enchantment: Theology, Poetics, and Social Change* (Richmond, IN: Bethany Theological Seminary, 2003).
7. Find an overview of this movement by visiting the website of the National Network Opposing the Militarization of Youth (http://www.nnomy.org) or the Youth and Militarism program of the American Friends Service Committee (http://www.youth4peace.org). A strategic treatment of the movement can be found in Matt Guynn, "Notes Toward More Powerful Organizing: Pitfalls and Potentials in Counter-recruitment Organizing," *Nonviolent Social Change: The Bulletin of the Manchester College Peace Studies Institute*, May 2008.
8. This model was developed with the collaboration of Deb Oskin. For a sample agenda, contact me at mguynn@onearthpeace.org.
9. This understanding of the demonic was informed by the work of Walter Wink. See his *Powers* trilogy, particularly *Unmasking the Powers* (Minneapolis: Augsburg Fortress, 1986).
10. For more on an elicitive approach to social change, please refer to the work of Training for Change, an international social change training center based in Philadelphia, Pennsylvania, which equips activists in effective facilitation and workshop leadership. I am a member of their training team. See http://www.trainingforchange.org.
11. This kind of social action research, and related elements that we brought into our organizing, were especially informed by Kingian nonviolence, and the work of David Jehnsen and Bernard LaFayette Jr., especially *The Leaders Manual — A Structured Guide & Introduction to Kingian Nonviolence: The Philosophy and Methodology*, by Bernard LaFayette Jr., and David C. Jehnsen (Galena, OH: Institute for Human Rights and Responsibilities). See http://www.kingiannonviolence.info.
12. Cited in *Original Goodness*, by Eknath Easwaran, founder of the Blue Mountain Center of Meditation, copyright 1989, 1996; reprinted by permission of Nilgiri Press, Tomales, CA, p. 11, http://www.easwaran.org.
13. Personal conversation, August 21, 2009. Thank you to Carol and conversation partners Karen Fraser Gitlitz, Ann Hunstiger, Tristan Bach and Mary Follen, all fellow students with me at the Grünewald Guild during my 2009 sabbatical. The Guild is an ecumenical Christian community in the mountains near Leavenworth, Washington, with the mission to "promote and encourage creativity within individuals and congregations in response to the mystery of creation through the exploration of art & faith." The Guild offers a variety of art instruction, retreat and travel programs. Visit the Grünewald Guild online at http://www.artfaith.com.

A THEOPOETICS OF THE BODY
Birth, Ecstasy, Emptying, Place, and Death

Patty Christiena Willis

Birth

Incarnation

On December 10th, 2004, a taxi took me from Varanasi to Bodh Gaya. I only had two hours to visit the place where the Buddha attained enlightenment. When I stepped out of the taxi, a man in an old jacket and a quarter-inch beard bowed in my direction and said urgently, "Please, Madame, let me be your guide." As a ploy, he acted as if I had already hired him and told me about a month-long celebration forty-eight years before. That was when I discovered what else was happening on the day my mother was being shaved (she said that was the worst part) and given a spinal block (that was the best part) as she prayed hard for my safety and perfection, feeling the contractions in her marrow. Her hands on her swollen stomach (she would never say belly) almost stretched to breaking, she felt my insistence to be released. Her hands firm above me, she prayed.

The man's cuffs had been reversed and stitched back on, as had his collar. My grandmother had taught me that trick from the depression. "Shirts can last twice as long," she said, showing me how to remove the collar with a seam ripper. His shoes had also been repaired, re-stitched and resoled. When I said, "Please be my guide," he smiled and the anxiety in his voice turned to pride. "Let us start at the corner of the complex," he said. "Forty-eight years ago," he said again, "there was a month-long celebration. It was May, at the time of the full moon. Twenty-five hundred years since the Buddha's birth. Can you imagine?" He looked over at me and raised his eyes to heaven. "Priests gathered from all over the world. Orange, brown, black, and yellow robes. It was a celebration of flowers. And elephants."

I was counting. "Did you say May 1956?" I asked.

"Yes," he said, "around the days of the waxing to the full moon and waning to a sliver." A crescendo and decrescendo of prayer.

Years before, I had seen a flower-covered elephant on a full moon night in Madurai. I thought that if I followed the elephant, I would arrive at god's garden. But, I couldn't. My shoes were held captive by the shoekeeper at the temple. No leather allowed. Why didn't I run barefoot through the city, a spectacle, spectacular in the flowered cotton dress I had made especially for that trip? Finally, I grabbed my shoes, a calculated risk, and left the shoekeeper's cubbyhole, his high voice threatening, "Madame, I will follow." Outside, the elephant has gone.

I forgot that night in Madurai until the guide's voice hushed and he said something about elephants covered in flowers and I heard: "Flowered elephants dancing on prayers." I didn't ask him to repeat. The part I wanted to be sure of was the date. "Yes," he said, calculating on his fingers, "May 1956." And he cocked his head and went on about the stupas of the compound and their age and historical significance.

When my mother closed her eyes between contractions, the anesthesia deliciously dulling the pain, her hands above me, still enclosed in her womb but traveling out, she blessed me and prayed. Amniotic fluid in my ears, did I hear her unspoken words and with them, underneath them, around them, as whales hear each other thousands of miles away, was there a faint chanting, drums drumming, voices urging elephants to keep circling the ground? Did the sea transmit, carry, sound waves from the other side of the earth? Could I hear like I heard the sea later, my ear to the wide lip of a conch?

When I asked about the size of the moon on my night of birth, my father said, "It was dark when we left the hospital. There must have been stars or a moon. It was May. But I don't remember the size of the moon, its waxing or waning. I was too busy praying thanks for your mother's safety and the perfection of your ten toes."

On December 26th, 2004, five days after I left India, a tsunami hit the coast near Chennai where I had clinked glasses at a fancy resort hotel. Did my feet feel it coming when I left the party, abandoning my shoes under the table and walking until I was ankle-deep in the sea? Did the imprints of my feet stay until the great wave came that swept the tables and beach umbrellas and buildings far out to sea?

How closely is our incarnation connected with others, how connected are our bodies to the Earth? It has been said that in death the body loses the weight of a dime. Does that weight, equal to what one can find on sidewalks or flip in the air, come from here and there? Is it parts of stars that are parts of other places and other people, parts of heaven, parts of the garden, all held together with *ruah*, the breath of life? Is our incarnation formed of places and people we remember in our dreams? Do we sometimes recognize our origins in what we see on travels and from the corners of our eyes on passing trains?

If we are lucky, our life began in an ecstasy of love. I am too shy to ask if this is true of mine.

Ecstasy

My own began with my elbow barely touching Mary Lou's. From that tiny point, ecstasy spread through my entire body until I felt beyond what I could bear. The whole night, I willed my body completely and totally still. Except at one point, which I later thought was a test, when Mary Lou moved her elbow slightly away. Mine followed like a magnet after a shift in the core of the Earth.

Snow falling outside our window, the infinity sign drew itself around our bodies and hovered above us: a holy blessing on our heads.

All of the particles that make up my body, and the *ruah* I call the breath of life, mysteriously, understandably, pulled me into the orbit of this woman, whose mother named her Mary Lou. The energy fields around us accepted each other as if we were made up of the perfect complement of stars and minerals. Wisely, we didn't speak of it. Without words, we felt its wonder travel over and through our skin into every corner of every cell.

This union did not happen at our first meeting; it was a dance that lasted for weeks until, exhausted, we lay side by side. On January 8, 1978, the day after I arrived in Paris, I went to church. So did Mary Lou.

It was the only time we had ever been in the same place at the same time or, to our knowledge, would have been. That church was the tiny intersection point of our very different worlds. After an acquaintance introduced us it was natural that we would sit together during the meeting, side by side. It was soon clear to her that I was devout but it wasn't clear to me for a very long time that she was not. She was in Paris to study music composition and I was there to teach and write.

The next week, she was not there. Someone said, "She is sick." I visited her with whole chocolate milk and pastries. I heated the milk on her Camping Gaz stove and together we sat drinking cocoa, buttery crumbs collecting on our laps from the *pain au chocolat.* "I like Emily Dickinson," she said. "So do I," said I.

Emily's words became a common ground between us, a place where we could meet and talk. After dinner (usually some kind of heavy casserole and *haricots verts)* at my *pension* on the edge of the Luxembourg Gardens, I searched for poems (in the complete works of Emily Dickinson that I had brought with me all the way to France) and copied them onto cards. The next day, I took the metro, changing trains once, to where she lived. If she wasn't home, I'd push the poetry under her door.

She had written songs to some of the poems. She had a cassette. One night in late January, we listened. The radiator hissed below her window that looked out on other old brick buildings too dark to see. The window mirrored us: Mary Lou on her bed and I in a chair, entranced. Her music held Emily's words in its arms and like ribbons they wove around us and then pulled tight.

A week later, on a trip to Mont St. Michel, staying in an *auberge* below the abbey, the snow falling outside our window, our elbows touched.

Only a knife could separate us, but who would wield it? The man I called Heavenly Father said, "I."

Emptying

Can emptying only happen after the experience of ecstasy? I do not know the order of the universe, only my own. My first experience of emptying happened falsely as a robbery in the night. After I left Mary Lou in London, after six months together in Paris, Heavenly Father gave me his knife in a dream:

I held the memory of being Abraham at the altar, raising his knife, only instead of an angel who pointed at the ram, God directed my knife to a place in her body and said, "Slice her there." He paused, "And while you are at it, slice yourself." And he guided my hand to the place within me that could be killed without taking my life. Abraham was lucky. He was blessed with a ram.

Then, a sleep came over us and the angel closed up the skin, like God did after he took out Adam's rib, suturing the wound above the cutting with such fine stitches we would doubt the memory of the sacrifice. We would think of the pain as "phantom pain" and convince ourselves that the memory of the altar and the knife had only been a dream.[1]

The true emptying came much later. It happened the summer I studied the ceremony for tea. There are two main schools. I did not study either. My friend, Yu-sensei, a priest, was the only teacher I could have, and she knew an entirely different school called Sohen Ryu. Her son, Shuho, was living at the house, waiting for the truth of his future to come clear. The Pure Land Sect makes it hard to discern. Staying on the middle road, with meat on one's plate, and a ready laugh, makes it much more difficult.

It was during our lessons that Yu-sensei taught us, "Shinran said that to be stupid is Buddha's Way." Had twenty years of linguistic and cultural predicaments not been in vain? Shuho and I listened as we learned to make tea.

Speaking the refined language of tea, politeness transforms giving into humbly receiving. In turn, hosts describe the act of receiving tea by the guests as giving. The ceremony is conducted on our knees. Tea is a cycle of emptying and filling, giving that is receiving and receiving that is giving.

Together, sometimes every day, the three of us gathered to study tea. As I learned the gestures, the way I moved transformed into the ceremony. Eating was a gentle reminder of its movement. Bathing, folding a towel, washing my body: all of it was tea. One day when I sat, at last not waiting for the moment when I put the powdered tea into the cup, or cleaned the utensils, or bowed as I placed the tea bowl in front of

Shuho, it happened in a flash. I was in that moment, in that moment. I emptied. Miraculously, I continued with the ceremony all the way to the second cup of tea for Yu-sensei and a sweet from Matsui-san's shop in the shape of a miniature hydrangea puffed full of bean paste.

It took years to fill. That summer, Shuho emptied too and his emptiness sent him to study to become a priest. Did my emptiness bring me to a seminary? He was hoping that I would become a priest too. He taught me to chant, and that summer, he painted beautiful lanterns to release the spirits of the dead. We let them go on the lake and filmed them bobbing on the water at dusk before we reeled them back in.

Over and over, I empty and fill and empty and fill. Will I ever reach a point where the state of emptying continues, when there is no filling up? Is that what they say is a good death? Or is that what they call the spirit of tea?

Place

Light in the Woods

How can you live
in that lonely place
for so many years?
In a lightning path.
Pelted with hail.
Buried in snow
and baked slowly by a hot sun?
Years are made of seasons
and seasons days.
Every day the wind
does not threaten
to blow me off the road,
I walk into the forest.
And each day my heart pounds
As if I'm on my way to meet a lover.
What scent will she wear?
How will the light dance on her neck and arms?
Will frost sparkle on her delicate feet?

In early evening,
A forest clearing
Slowly fills with gold
From the setting sun.
In that clearing only once,
She danced.[2]

Almost ten years to the day after our move to Japan, we found our place on Earth. I first saw the house in my dreams, its heavy handhewn beams holding up delicate walls made of woven bamboo and pressed earth. The house was waiting on the edge of destruction and as we held out our hands it caught us in its arms.

I fell in love as I opened the heavy doors and stepped into the entryway, dust particles dancing in the light from a high window. Mary Lou ran to the back of the house and listened to the trees. I think we heard *ruah* in that place. The breath of God called us to stay.

Until that moment, I had called many different places in the world "home" but I had not *felt* home like that before: the old house was a sounding board and my ear against it, I tuned my body to the heartbeat of the earth.

Near the spot where Mary Lou listened to the trees, we planted a garden. In the spring, we tilled the earth until our backs were tired and we took our picnics there. Spreading a blanket under the blooming mountain cherry trees on the hillside below our garden, we dined. And then sleepy and full, we stretched out on the earth for a nap. I think that the garden wed us in our sleep, a lusty bridegroom with two wives. Our hearts leaned in his direction so much that early in the morning we left our cozy bed with sickles and shovels and hoes. We braved the insects of summer and the typhoons of autumn and even in the winter, our bridegroom could call to us from under the snow. One afternoon, hungry for chard sweetened by the cold, we crawled over the deep snow to dig our hands deep into his heart and harvest the black green leaves. And it was the best soup of the winter, in a chicken broth with spices and sour cream.

For the inhabitants, the village was their ancestral home. When I pointed out the beauty, they said, "I never thought of it quite that way." When I spoke of digging in the earth, they told me about a lonely mushroom farmer on the other side of the mountain who would love someone like me for a wife.

The villagers planted and harvested rice and vegetables for their livelihood but their duty was to care for the family grave. After ten years, during which they lost the sense that we strangers would be going home, they began to worry about us. "Where are your graves?" they asked as they passed our house with bouquets. One grave held the whole family: the war dead, the very old and the children who had gone too soon. Each grave had a place for flowers that was almost always full. In the early winter, camellia bushes presided from above and in mid-winter, narcissus bloomed wildly at the foot of the mound chosen for their dead. We thought and thought about the location of our grave and pointed at a place to the side of our field, "Maybe we will be buried just over there." Strangely, at the moment we knew that this piece of earth would accept us in death we began to yearn for another home, for a place where our own ancestors may have passed in a wagon or planted a blackberry bush in the wild.

When we decided to leave, I stopped touching the earth around our house. We didn't visit our bridegroom for fear that he would grab our hands and hold us in a dance. Tilling the earth had tied us to that place and its bounty had fed us, its flowers had graced our lives. Its landscape had become the landscape of our hearts and the path through the woods became our path to God. It was there we saw the forest dance in the light.

Death

A pilgrimage to India took me north to Rishikesh. I sat on the banks of the Ganges, clear at its source in the mountains. By the sparkling water, I listened to a woman tell her story during an afternoon gathering called a *satsang*. "She is enlightened," they whispered and I listened. The man seated next to me doubted and wanted to take me with him to a restaurant for a beer. I stayed. "Look up at the trees," she said. "The leaves are moving. Whatever happens in your life, look up at the trees and see the leaves."

That night I ate *dal* and *chapattis* at the hostel restaurant. Satya, whose name means truth, sat with me. She told me that she was forgetting many details of her life. At seventy, she had come to India to ask about her memory loss. That afternoon, a wise man had told her to let the past go. She smiled at me. The man had brought her happy news.

"Come with me," she said and together we walked out into the darkness and listened to the river below. "When my daughter had problems, I told her to look up at the stars." We looked up at the sky full of stars. "You are safe when you can see the stars."

In the morning, I received news that the bus companies were planning to strike. If I didn't leave for Delhi that morning, I would not make my flight home. I packed my belongings and bundling into a three-wheeled taxi, and I sped alongside the holy river for the bus station of Haridwar. I stepped out of the taxi and strode into the station. As I crossed the wide-open space, a tall man picked me up in his arms and carried me out of the trajectory of a bus. When we reached safely, he put me down and turning to me, he pressed his hands together. "*Namaste*," he said and disappeared.

That day, I began anew. "I have been given one more hour, one more day," I thought on the twelve-hour bus ride back to Delhi, waiting another twelve hours in the Indira Gandhi International Airport and four hours to Bangkok and more waiting (but I was too tired to count) and then eight hours to Narita. Everything late, late, late, I missed my flight home and had to go into Tokyo, spend a night at the Tokyo Station Hotel and take a train through a hundred tunnels (they say) that make the trip to western Japan only 5 instead of 10 hours long. I was alive. Mary Lou was alive and waiting for me. The cherry trees were in full bloom across the pond from our house. My first morning when we ate breakfast on our porch, a wind came up from Deep Valley and lifted the cherry blossoms up off the trees in a great blossom cloud that flew up and up and then dispersed. Petals fell into our open hands.

The weeks before I went to India, I had fallen into pieces. In India I put them together again. And there I would have died if that one tall man had not seen me and acted. He had risked his own life to rescue mine. When Buddhists of the Pure Land sect die, their families dress them in the robes of a pilgrim. They slip fake money into the robe's pocket for the boatman of the Sanzu River. The money gives the pilgrim a chance to reach the other side.

Many times, people, sometimes complete strangers, have handed me the currency I needed to move ahead. Only weeks ago, after experiencing a personal tragedy that tore my world to pieces again, I sat with a

Quaker healer. In his gentle presence, I released my grief and when he asked me for a word to describe my present state, I said, "Transformation."

He said, "Do you know that when John baptized Jesus, he held him under the water for so long that he gasped for air and literally fought for his life?" I closed my eyes and took a dive downward into the water while staying in my chair. "Baptism is different than people think," he said. "You do not return to the place on the bank where you started; you cross the River Jordan to the other side." I struggled out of the water and headed to the other side of the shore. "When you get there a voice calls out, 'Behold my beloved daughter in whom I am well pleased.'" I cried unashamedly, listening to the voice. "And there on the bank, you will find new clothes to wear. A new life has begun."

In the ending, there is a beginning. Is there baptism in death and a walk or swim or boat ride to the other side? I do not know for sure what happens, but I know that there is movement. We are here and then we are there. We are in pieces and then we are whole.

Notes

1. From my memoirs, *A True Story of Bilingual Cats.*
2. Patty Willis. "Light in the Woods," a poem from the CD *Light in the Woods.* Christiena Prince Workshop. 2005.

SALMONEUS AND THE POETS
Poetry in a World of Violence

Travis Poling

A reading from the book, *Gods, Demigods and Demons*:[1]
Salmoneus, King of Elis and brother of Sisyphus, shared his elder brother's contempt for the gods. Salmoneus grew so arrogant that he commanded his subjects to address him as "Zeus." To validate his claim to divine honors, he clanged iron pots together calling it thunder and hurled torches into the night sky to mimic lightning. Zeus, of course, viewed such pretensions with enormous displeasure, which he expressed by hurling a thunderbolt at Salmoneus, killing him instantly. After his death, Salmoneus was consigned to a part of Hades near where his brother, Sisyphus, was undergoing his own special torment. As Salmoneus observed his brother's ordeal, turnspit demons were basting him over a flame so that he sizzled through eternity as his brother eternally rolled his rock.

This story[2] shows us how Salmoneus, who "hurled torches into the night sky," might serve as a metaphor for the poet in a world of violence. Through his action of launching light through the darkness, this king was doing more than assaulting an already angry god. He was asserting his vision of a world without violence sanctioned from above and allowing others to share in what he saw: that the gods of violence are always a threat to human sensibilities. It is true that this king claimed divinity for himself, but so too do poets, and all mortals, at least to the extent that humans can be divine—that is, to live in the image of the One who created us. But Zeus did not create the people of Greece.

He merely ruled over them like an angry father, much like human distortions of the God of Abraham, Jesus, and Mohamed, as the one who could be called Mighty Destroyer. Zeus represents here the spirits of outrage, hatred, slavery, torture, retribution, and war. Salmoneus, like the poet, is one who knows the truth, that such power can only take the god so far, and so challenges Mount Olympia with flame and iron, symbols of light and strength crafted by human hands. Being a god of quick tempers, Zeus lashes out with lightning, a real threat to human flesh, leaving Salmoneus victim to the spirits of violence. And the dead king's suffering does not end there. He is sentenced to helplessly watch his brother Sisyphus, enslaved for his own challenge to the gods, roll a boulder uphill, only to have it tumble back down each time he nears the summit. Simultaneously, Salmoneus himself is tortured, in tragic irony, in flame upon an iron rod.

Poetry enables vision, a particular way of seeing the world as it truly is. It removes the mask that humanity dons to hide from the gravity of life amidst doldrums, brokenness, anxiety, violence, and death and reveals the bitter—and the joyous—truth: we are alienated yet united, unfeeling yet tearful, frightened yet courageous, violent yet loving, dead yet alive. Life contains all of these dichotomies, and we never know which part of it we will be in next: a new day may bring joy that the pain of yesterday is past, a healthy infant may live through her first night while the next may perish before he is born, and a hurricane may come one day and the full sun the next. Life is unstable and unpredictable, for that is what vibrancy is. If life were the same thing continually, there would be nothing vibrant about anything. We would cease to seize the day and begin to let it drop through our ever weakening hands; or, in the case of the suffering brother of Salmoneus and all poets, off our eternally aching backs. For Zeus, for the spirits that feed on flesh, this is power. And so the poet, the artist and lover of life, lives to hurl flame into the deep darkness where violence reigns and lightning sings terror in the heart of the earth. But this flame is not the fire of the arsonist threatening heaven. It is the light that shines in the darkness. And the darkness will never overcome it, as long as there are poets with torches.

In the spirit of Salmoenus, I offer three original poems from my own arsenal of torches. May we be blessed in our hearing of these words.

She Stands, Still Weeping

    Her caravan moves swiftly
    across the plain, away
    from the city, away
    from home. All her past,
    possessions, confidants,
    confessions that define her

    are aflame. How could she
    not stop, not glance—eyes
    overflowing, salt on her tongue,
    tears down her cheeks, shoulders.
    The morning passes, and then
    the day, tears still streaming
    down her skin, dripping

    into her pores. Months, years,
    a decade of shock, of realizing
    why and weeping, flesh absorbing
    a mother's salt of sorrows—
    corrosion from the epiphany
    that unveils corruption
    turns all mothers into monuments

    of tears, reminding God of sorrow.
    At least someone is mourning as only
    a mother can—of course her husband
    does not stop, does not wonder how
    that pillar got there. Only she can

    say why her home was destroyed
    in sulphur; only Lot's wife knows
    God's secret; it whispers in her heart,
    as she shouts back, "Far be that from you!"
    That is why she turned, why
    she stands, still weeping, and
    why the pillar grows steadily.

Eastern Market Metro Station, Washington, DC

> A woman offered me her body
> one night, under the streetlight
> outside the train, her dim eyes
> clutching sorrow. In this city
> I fight against war, but can not resist
> the clash in her eyes, peering into mine
> for dignity, for happiness, for one night
> without hunger because I might
>
> fill her or take her, either way touch her
> heart to mine. As dollars pass from my hands
> to hers—"Have this instead"—we exchange glances—
> a different kind of currency. It is the smaller tokens
> we trade: a glance, standing still, hand touching
> hand saying, "Take—eat."

This Is What Saves The Valley

> Some people, too many young, have tossed their lives
> > from High Rock
> without sails on their backs, without hope in their bellies.
> They leap into this valley to cross its abyss to God, but
> God does not hold them up, cannot suspend bodies in air,
> even where air is alive enough to fly on.
>
> I remember the valley every single day, its full moons and half ones,
> its Cassiopeia—our exiled, inverted queen of heavens, shimmering
> prayers of solace from her center star.
> I have never forgotten what it means to live nestled, ringed
> by blue ridges deeper than the sky that hang-gliders soar into
> and farther down, deep where the red oaks pull in their sap,
> tossing their leaves, their lives.
>
> Cumberland Valley is paradise, I say, but that does not
> > strike out death.

Too often the young cannot see its visions, even from vistas.
        They leap into beauty,
eyes soundly shut. The world sends clouds too heavy
        to gaze through,
splitting people from this vibrant swale, even while the sun
        glances down,
a warm blaze through harvest rains.

Eve and Adam invented death, were exiled from their land
and I sympathize, living as I do on top of the earth with Hoosiers.
Even the highest point in Indiana is barely a slope; to jump would
        deliver you
straight back down on your feet that cannot fly in that box of a land.
The valley is a crescent, like that fertile sickle of a land
where Eden was plowed over like Indiana is plowed,
        and plowed—and plowed.

What saves the valley is the hills on rollercoaster roads that lift
your solar plexus from your seat, praise God for seat belts
        and padded car ceilings.
What saves the valley is the land holding us up, never bowing
        to serve us.
We build our houses, our roads, our orchards and dairies around
        the land,
our churches near streams for immersion baptisms, leaving water
        off in the baptistery
to wade in real waters, waters you can feel in the bones of your
        bones, swift and cool.
Creeks do not flow in the valley, they run like bucks in rut,
        butting station wagons,
wide elms, and women. Mountains can do wonders for
        momentum, and force,
and gentleness, and peace, and prayer, and shouting. Because the
        mountains
shout back, you know the earth hears every single tree that falls
        in her woods.
Because of the valley, tumbling bodies always make a sound.

Travis Poling is pursuing a Master of Arts in Worship Studies at Bethany Theological Seminary in Richmond, Indiana. These three poems will be published in an upcoming chapbook, *Poems That Should Never Be Read in Church*, available at http://www.travispoling.com.

Notes

1. Bernard Evslin. *Gods, Demigods and Demons: A Handbook of Greek Mythology.* I.B. Tarius, New York: 2006, 190.

2. This article was originally presented at Bethany Theological Seminary's Presidential Forum, March 30, 2009.

POMEGRANATE

Jean Janzen

We live in a valley of Biblical fruits. Grapes, figs, olives, and pomegranates thrive in this subtropical climate. The soil of an ancient seabed combined with hot summers and the irrigation of mountain snows combines into a fertile setting.

In our own garden, a lovely, gnarled fig tree spreads its many arms and large, rough leaves, then supplies us and the birds with at least three crops of pale pink succulence every summer. Even our neighborhood fox jumps up for the ripest ones. Our one pomegranate tree offers its sweetness in autumn, the weighty balls of rosy skin clinging to the branches of lacy leaves as the seeds gather sugar until their pouches split, ripening just in time to be placed in honor on our Thanksgiving and Christmas tables.

Our first pomegranates in Fresno arrived as a gift to my pediatrician husband, a shopping bagful. What to do with these unfamiliar globes? "Cut them open and suck out the juice," my husband said, as he stood over the sink in a kind of rapture. Suck and chew and spit out the seeds in primal joy. The children were enthralled while I somewhat carefully let my teeth sink in to release the astringency, this juice that is both sweet and tart. When I discovered that the splattered stains were almost impossible to remove, the new rule in the house was for the children to take off their clothes and sit in the bathtub to eat this strange fruit.

The seeds are bright jewels in a leather-like cup, divided into sections of white parchment. Amazing and ancient. I fell in love, and each year press them for juice to drink and to make jelly. Other times

I meticulously remove the seeds for salads. The grandchildren remind me each year to make their favorite Jello salad, which features the seeds whole, softened enough in the gel to swallow them. And at Christmas, I send home with them a jelly jar of this exotic fruit, each spoonful like a large ruby on bread or waffles.

Fruit of mythology. In the Greek myth of Persephone, the pomegranate is called the fruit of the underworld. Persephone is persuaded to swallow one seed, resulting in the requirement that she returns into the dark earth for a part of every year. Pliny offers advice on preserving this fruit by hardening them in seawater, then drying them in the sun for 3 days. Homer places the tree into his Garden of Alcinous. In the Muslim Qu'uran, it is called the fruit of Paradise.

It is the Biblical source that intrigues me most. The tree is mentioned in Haggai, Song of Solomon, Deuteronomy, Numbers, First Samuel, and especially Exodus. In the instructions for the Tabernacle, pomegranates are to be attached to the hem of the priests: "They made pomegranates of blue, purple, and scarlet yarn and finely twisted linen around the hem of the robe. And they made bells of pure gold and put the bells between the pomegranates all around on the hem of the robe, alternating a bell and a pomegranate all around on the hem of the robe for the service, just as the Lord had commanded Moses." This instruction with its repetitive phrasing sounds like a song or poem, lifting the fruit into textile art, exciting the senses as they shimmer between the ringing golden bells. The High Priest enters the Holy of Holies through the dyed curtains, the elements of earth crafted into beauty and swinging around his feet.

What has this to do with a Mennonite woman taught to live simply and frugally? My lessons in preservation of fruits and vegetables began when I was tall enough to lean over the kitchen counter to peel and slice, hours at a time. It was tedious, and it was the way of winter survival—corn, peaches, peas, beans, tomatoes, and even chicken. The gleaming jars were carried into the cellar to which my mother's friends were invited to view the harvest behind glass.

Canning changed to freezing when I moved to this valley, and soon fresh produce was available year around. I have the luxury to choose, sometimes slicing luscious peaches for frozen pie fillings, or crushing the figs for jam, and every year I am willing to stand by the sink to patiently remove the seeds and press the halves of pomegranates for juice. Sometimes I experiment with sauces for pork and chicken. And now the fruit is a super-healthy one. Loaded with antioxidants, we can "drink and live," if we pay.

I have the Jesuit missionaries to thank for bringing the trees to California. With these trees, they brought the rule of the Catholic Church. Grace and beauty, but with boundaries. For the Jews, the fruit is a symbol of the Torah—613 seeds in each pomegranate for the 613 commandments. Such numbers remind me of the hours of slicing and peeling, and of the need for preservation. Litany and liturgy, the daily prayers, what nourishes and saves. But I also think about the knife cutting through when I divide the fruit into halves, 306 and a half commandments in each section, which I crush in my pomegranate squeezer, then pour out the brilliant juice into a cup and drink—one-half for the first commandment of fulfillment: "Thou shalt love the Lord thy God with all thy heart and soul and mind," and the other half for the second, "and thy neighbor as thyself."

POETRY

JEAN JANZEN

PSALM 91

Under the attic rafters my sister and I
played house, our dolls naked and stiff
in our arms as we dressed them.
Summer rain drumming overhead,
rumble of thunder. Don't be afraid,
we lisped, and sang into the small
curve of their ears, wrapped the blanket
tighter. Little girls mothering our dolls'
stares into sleep, their eyelids closing
as we lowered them into shoe box beds.
"He shall give his angels charge
over thee," we chanted into the solemn
air of the wartime 40s, "to keep
thee in all thy ways," as somewhere
far away bodies fell under burning planes,
children stumbled and screamed
for cover. Did we sing for ourselves
or for those dead who lay in broken
streets, where they no longer heard
the rumble, their eyes wide open
under the shadow of the Almighty.

POETRY

JEAN JANZEN

WRITING THE FIRE

Child with crayon draws
one line, then another, a curve,
and finally, the circle of O,
our story in alphabet.
Shelter of H for house with smoke
rising. Capital I, the column
on which we teeter, unless
we bend, arms open to the other.
Write it, that sizzle toward embrace,
words that lean into each other, then
pull away in patterns of flicker
and glow until all is given up to air.
*
I write "Ash Wednesday,"
give title to my body's burning.
Now in this valley's cusp of spring,
first stirrings in the vineyard
where the vintner chose two stems
and tied them to the wire, bound
to drink the roots and dawn, for
the miracle of leaf unfolding,
and for the grape's green kernel.
Write it, that slow swelling toward
ripeness, and the crush, which
we sip and swallow into smoldering.
*
I sleep with Psalms beside my head,
the pages luminous with pain and praise.
My dreams wander in the wilderness
where manna is hidden, and I wake,
starved for the day's gifts:

husband breathing beside me,
my body's power to turn, to stand,
and walk into another morning.
Write it, the hunger and the song—
the bee in patterns of search and honey,
amber and gold now lacing
this shallow river of hours.

CONTRIBUTORS

Crystal Downing is Professor of English and Film Studies at Messiah College. Her book, *Writing Performances: The Stages of Dorothy L. Sayers*, was recently honored in Cambridge, England with the first Barbara Reynolds Award for outstanding Sayers scholarship.

David Harris Ebenbach's first book of short stories, *Between Camelots*, won the Drew Heinz Literature Prize and the GLCA New Writer's Award. His short stories and poems have been published in numerous journals and collections. He teaches Creative Writing at Earlham College.

Jeff Gundy has published five books of poems and three of prose, including *Spoken Among the Trees*. He is Professor of English at Bluffton University and was the 2008 Fulbright Lecturer in American Studies at the University of Salzburg.

Matt Guynn is a poet, peace educator, and activist working for the organization On Earth Peace. His previous work on theopoetics and social transformation has appeared in *CrossCurrents*.

L.B. Callid Keefe-Perry is an educator, artist, and poet. He is the webmaster of *theopoetics.net* and an emerging scholar in the genre of theopoetics. He is a traveling minister within, and beyond, the Religious Society of Friends and has served as a teacher of Quakerism at Pendle Hill.

Jean Janzen's latest book of poems is *Paper House*, her seventh collection. She has taught poetry writing at Fresno University and Eastern Mennonite University and is now working on memoir essays.

Ruthann Knechel Johansen is president of Bethany Theological Seminary and professor emerita of the University of Notre Dame where she taught in the Program of Liberal Studies and was a fellow at the Kroc Institute of International Peace Studies. Her book, *The Narrative Secret of Flannery O'Connor: The Trickster As Interpreter*, has just been reissued by the University of Alabama Press.

David L. Miller is Watsen-Ledden Professor of Religion Emeritus at Syracuse University and a retired Core Faculty Member at Pacifica Graduate Institute in Santa Barbara. His many publications include *Hells and Holy Ghosts: A Theopoetics of Christian Belief*.

Travis Poling is a poet and seminary student. In addition to his work in liturgy and ministry studies, he is at work on a study of the poet William Stafford.

Patty Christiena Willis is known in Japan for her youth novel *The Village Above the Stars*, published in Japanese and recommended by the Library Association of Japan. Her theater work has been performed internationally and her play *Yugetsu* received a national playwriting award.

www.ingramcontent.com/pod-product-compliance
Lightning Source LLC
Chambersburg PA
CBHW040300170426
43193CB00020B/2952